THE PASTOR'S SURVIVAL KIT

THE PASTOR'S SURVIVAL KIT

A Wealth of Resource Material

Vada Lee Barkley

Copyright © 2003 by Vada Lee Barkley.

ISBN: Softcover   1-4134-0086-8

All rights reserved. No part of this book may be reproduced or transmitted in any form or by any means, electronic or mechanical, including photocopying, recording, or by any information storage and retrieval system, without permission in writing from the copyright owner.

This book was printed in the United States of America.

To order additional copies of this book, contact:
Xlibris Corporation
1-888-795-4274
www.Xlibris.com
Orders@Xlibris.com
18376

CONTENTS

Preface 7
Introduction 9
Chapter 1
    Devotional Material 11
Chapter 2
    Sample Sermons from the Past 29
Chapter 3
    Food for Thought 66
Chapter 4
    Anecdotes 83
Chapter 5
    Outlines 99
Chapter 6
    Thoughts on Prayer 110
Chapter 7
    Insights into the Word 118
Chapter 8
    Red Flag Alert 127
Chapter 9
    Hints for Improving Relationships 146
Chapter 10
    A Crash Course in Communications 161

PREFACE

Like most preachers, my late husband, Rev. Arthur E. Barkley, searched the Scriptures and every other available source pertaining to them. He studied the works of almost every outstanding preacher of the past. And he heard many of them preach.

Not only did he serve as a pastor and an evangelist for years, but he also served as a lay pastor and hospital chaplain. He taught the Bethel Bible series and two different Sunday school classes in the largest church in our denomination. *The Pastor's Survival Kit* contains several chapters of excerpts from his notes compiled over a period of 65-70 years.

INTRODUCTION

If I know anything about preachers, and I should—I have taught them;
   counseled them;
      edited their books and dissertations;
         spent the equivalent of four years with more than one hundred different parsonage families;
            had at least 25 different pastors;
               heard a minimum of 100,000 sermons;
                  been a preacher's wife for over 50 years; taken one international student into our home and taught him basic English. After graduating from seminary, he accepted a pastorate where he has been for 22 years.

Now I regularly attend 3 monthly meetings composed primarily of retired ministers and their spouses. For no group do I have more love and respect.

If I know anything about preachers, I know they are always on the lookout for sermon material or anything that will help them in their ministry.

This book is designed to meet some of those needs.

CHAPTER 1

Devotional Material

If you know Christ, He has been the strength for your weakness, the comfort for your sorrow, the light for your darkness. His presence has been sufficient in hours when the heart and flesh were failing and trouble was knocking at your door.

If He, the Sun of Righteousness, has risen upon you with healing in His wings, then you hold in your possession the blessing for which this world in its pitiful condition is waiting. There never was a time when the need was greater for every Christian to witness vigorously by life, deed, and word to the power of the Christ whose name we bear.

If the church were witnessing with all her might, by all her members, to the things we most surely believe, how tremendous would be the impact on this perplexed generation!

If we, the children of Zion, whose captivity God has ended, had our mouths filled with songs of praise for the joy of our great deliverance, think of the shadows that would be flooded with the blessed light of hope!

A religious movement tends to follow a well defined pattern.

I. It begins as a minority, despised by the majority and hated if it continues to grow. Such a group is not tempted to seek popularity.
II. As the movement grows it gradually becomes rich and powerful. There comes the desire for standing and acceptance.

To foster this desire it begins to water down the stricter parts of its doctrine.

III. The question is no longer "Does the Lord command it?" But "What will influential people think?"

Everyone needs a refuge from four things in particular: from the power of the devil; from the accusations of conscience; from the fear of death; and from the wrath to come.

Many people trust in false refuges.

1. Some take refuge in the lie that God does not exist. Since atheism is a lie, it is foolish to try to find a refuge in it. God does exist and He will hold us accountable for sin.
2. Others take refuge in the lie that the Bible is not the Word of God; it is simply a collection of unreliable myths and legends. But nothing has ever been discovered that proved the Bible wrong; whereas thousands of proofs validate its truth.
3. Some take refuge in the lie that God is too good to damn anyone. Thus they believe that everyone is going to be saved.
4. Others believe that people are saved by their own morality rather than by the substitutionary work of Christ.
5. Many are taking refuge in the lie that one religion is as good as another. Thus it makes no difference what one believes so long as he is sincere. But Christianity is the only true religion; all others are false. If being religious was enough, Jesus Christ would not have insisted upon faith in Himself as the only way.
6. Some take refuge in the lie that after death sinners will have a second chance to accept Christ and be saved.

One of the most successful business men in Florida Gold Coast learned an amazing fact from the accounting firm that audited his books every year.

The accountant said, "I'm glad to see that your company tithes and that you personally tithe as well."

"Thank you," the business man answered. "I guess you're a tither too."

"No," said the accountant, "I don't really strictly tithe, but I ought to. I've been auditing books in Florida for over twenty years, and I have never seen a firm that tithes go bankrupt or get into serious financial trouble."

The business man said, "Say that again; it interests me."

The accountant took his glasses off and talked for twenty minutes naming some of the most successful business firms in Florida that were tithers.

George MacDonald said to a group of people he had noticed were anxious and hard-pressed, "It isn't being poor, and it isn't being rich, and it isn't even being good that can make you happy.

"You're like children sitting on the curbstone, hunting in the gutter for things. Behind you is a King's palace, finer than Buckingham, but you won't even listen to the messengers sent out to tell you that it's yours! You won't even turn around and look!

"You just keep hunting around in the gutter, and maybe it's pennies or just junk you find there. They can't make you happy without your Father."

Thornton Wilder tells of standing in front of a New York theater several years ago, watching thousands of teenagers, as they stood in the snow, waiting to see a certain young American rock singer.

Finally the singer arrived and was brought in through a rear door so he wouldn't be mobbed by these thousands of kids.

Inside the theater, he began his program. Immediately the teenagers reacted in typically American fashion. They screamed, they wept, they wailed, and they attempted to tear the singer's clothes off.

Looking on from the sidelines, Wilder wondered, *"Why all this wild demonstration?"* Then he came to the conclusion that our young people need something to adore, something to challenge them. That raised the question, "What is there left to adore in our modern world?"

Young people are looking for something big enough to live for and important enough to die for. A weak challenge will not gain their attention, much less their allegiance. Only Christ can meet that need.

There has never been anyone like Jesus on this earth. Twenty centuries have been looking at that majestic life with microscopic scrutiny and have yet to find one flaw, one moral failure, one unworthy deed He ever did. Christ is the perfect revelation.

I have seen the light that comes into human eyes with the birth of a genuine religious experience.

I have seen a person growing simply radiant, full of a new hope and peace and attractiveness through a discovery of what Jesus is and what He can do.

I have heard the simple testimony that everything has been different—home life, church life, personal relationships—since the day when Christ became real and made all things new.

I thank God that this transforming experience is within the reach of all.

God will take away even Death, this terrible enemy which digs graves and ruins hopes, then sails triumphantly over an ocean of tears. That carries presidents and princes, the wise and the beautiful to a bed in the dust and forces every friend to leave them there.

If there is any way I can conquer Death, let me know, for I dread him day and night. Thank God, there is!

Death is only the fording of the river to enter the portal of life where the weeping of friends is answered by the welcome of angels.

What the world dreads, the believer at last welcomes, for it takes him from pain to peace, from toil to rest, from age to youth, from death to life everlasting.

We are on our way to that which Christ has promised and Death only ushers us into our inheritance.

Thornton Wilder, in *Our Town,* pictures a girl returning from the land beyond the grave and saying something like this to her mother, "Mother, look at me! We never took time to look at each other when I was on earth!"

Then she sees other people she had known, but they can't see her. She wants to relive her fourteenth birthday. But it is all so miserable for her that she is glad to return to her place beyond this life. She wished she hadn't come back from the dead at all.

Just as the physical body I now have is what I need for living in a physical environment, the spiritual body that I shall have then will be what I shall need for the spiritual world where I shall be.

"To the saints of God," says Dr. Robert I. Hough, in *The Christian after Death,* "death is nothing to cause distress or sorrow or fear; for, while it does take the saints from things held dear, it brings them into an even more precious relationship."

Dr. F.B. Meyer, one of the great Christians of another generation, wrote to a friend on the day before his death. "I have just heard, to my surprise, that I have only a few days to live. It may be that before this reaches you I shall have entered the palace. Don't trouble to write. We will meet you in the morning. With much love, F.B. Meyer."

The Apostle Paul says that the death of the Christian is far better than being here. The spiritual body will not be subject to limitations, pain, or decay. The treasure laid up will be available.

Sin and death will be banished. And, above all, the believer will be ushered into the presence of God and the host of saints who await him.

Ben Franklin wrote, "We are spirits. That bodies should be lent us so long as they can afford us pleasure, assist us in acquiring knowledge, or in doing good to our fellowman, is a kind and benevolent act of God. When they become unfit for these purposes, and afford us pain instead of pleasure, and instead of an aid become an incumbrance, it is equally kind and benevolent that a way is provided by which we may depart from them.

"Death is that way. It is as if our friend and we were invited to a house party, which is to last forever. His chair was ready first, and he has gone before us. We could not all conveniently start together. And we should not be grieved at this, since we some day will follow, and know where to find him."

Where the real center of life ought to be there is an empty space in the lives of many people. It can only be filled by God. Pascal, the physicist and philosopher, called it a "vacuum in the heart of every man which cannot be satisfied by any created thing." It can be satisfied only by God, the Creator, who is made known through Jesus Christ.

Isn't it amazing that after we wander through all the knowledge which has come to the world in the past centuries, we have to go back to the simple things which Jesus said and take what He taught as foundational?

When life breaks up and falls in on us, it has been the experience of His people that Jesus can restore everything for us. He can, and He does!

How important it is that the facts concerning the beginning of Christ's life on earth should be firmly established!

Fundamentally, all we know about Christ's life while here on earth, we learn from the four Gospels.

There are only two detailed accounts of the circumstances that surrounded our Lord's entrance into this world that have any historical value—the first two chapters of Matthew and the first two chapters of Luke.

The entrance of Christ into the world was, according to the gospel records, a supernatural event.

If the accounts are not true, we would say that these men had the mind of a fiction writer. But there is every reason for believing these stories.

If we take the Bible seriously it will show us that days of calamity, both personal and national, can be times of growing faith and increased knowledge of God.

The Bible often tells us of men who found God, or were found of God, when life went all to pieces for them.

Again and again in the Old Testament we find great souls dealing with God, or being dealt with by God, through hard trials and dark doubts.

Today, more than any other generation since Jeremiah, the prophet, people are saying, "Peace, peace, when there is no peace."

Even within families there is a peace-at-any-price attitude. The mother and children knuckle under a dictator type father whose word must be obeyed and whose opinions must not be questioned. Or the father and children submit to a domineering woman. Or the parents are actually so afraid of their children that they let the little tyrants have their own way just to keep peace in the family.

But peace begins in the human heart or it doesn't begin at all. Peace with God is secured and the regenerating power of Christ enters when Christ comes into our lives.

A popular psychology of success is presented from some pulpits in the name of religion. It is all about how to use God for the satisfaction of our own self interests, how to make Him an ally in our efforts to have personal popularity and business prosperity.

These claims are very pleasing to many congregations who call it good, down-to-earth preaching. The trouble is that it is down-to-earth, not up to God.

The thing that breaks hearts and fills graves is the fearful thing called sin. Sin conquered Samson, the strong; Saul, the warrior; Absalom, the fair; and Solomon, the wise. It conquered Antony and Cleopatra; Adolf Hitler; and Julian, the Apostate.

To say sin is negligible is self-deception. Sorrow, sin, and shame have not gone out of fashion. "The wages of sin is death" is as true today as it was more than two thousand years ago.

When the Honorable C.T. Wang, former ambassador to the United States from China, left Washington to return home, a newspaper reporter asked him what most impressed him about the United States.

He said, "What most impressed me was this: America is a Christian country and yet, though I came from a heathen land, no one in America has ever asked me to attend a Christian church or ever spoken to me about Christ."

Jesus lived in an ordinary neighborhood, such a neighborhood as thousands of hard-working people live in today. And His village was not held in high esteem by the people of neighboring villages. Upon hearing that a great prophet had come from that place, Nathaniel asked, "Can any good thing come out of Nazareth?"

The world in which He moved was not so much different from the world we know. He had the same problems we face. He made His living by a craft that is still important and honorable.

Jesus was a light to illumine evil, a voice to rebuke sin, but He was also a sign-post pointing men to God.

Think of the world as it was over two thousand years ago before the angels sang at Bethlehem. That proud imperial world which was beginning to be rotten to the core, festering with sin, and with all its gods dead, all its wisdom bankrupt, and all its morals in chaos.

Desperate voices were crying then out of the darkness, "Watchman, what of the night?" and weary eyes were straining in vain through the gloom for some indication of hope.

So it was when the fullness of time was come and God sent forth His Son.

Bronson Alcott was a philosopher. He spent a lot of time training young people.

One day he strolled into the village school. Often a visitor would be asked to make a few remarks. So Alcott stood up and looked the class over. Then he asked abruptly, "What do you come here for?"

Some giggled. Then one of the bolder boys said, "We come here to learn."

The philosopher pressed the question, "To learn what?"

That started them thinking. Finally one answered, "To learn to behave."

That was wiser than to have said, "To learn to multiply or to spell."

The whole curriculum of life might be condensed into those words.

The sum total of our learning might be said to be, "To learn to behave."

There's a vast difference between Christ's first coming and His second coming. First, He "came unto His own" knocking, a sign of weakness; came to His city—His triumphal entry—on a donkey; arose and took a towel and washed the disciples' feet; and died on Calvary. But John the Revelator describes a different coming: (1) He comes in power on a horse, not a donkey; (2) We will be at His feet; and (3) He will sit on a white throne.

We criticize people of a few generations back for their ignorance, but the past could criticize us for our indolence.

We may be able to travel faster than our forefathers, but are we any better people or any better prepared to perform our tasks than they were?

We never had so many laws and so much lawlessness. We never had so many fine homes and so many broken homes.

We have never had so many books on how to raise children, and so many bad children. We've never had so much talk about love and so much hate.

People always seem to want more than they have.

1. A man wants a better job.
2. His wife is not as attractive as he would like her to be.
3. The children are not geniuses.
4. The dog is not of the right pedigree.
5. The bank balance is too low.
6. The church he belongs to is dead.
7. His money is not worth what it used to be.
8. Young people today are not what they should be.
9. His wife is not affectionate enough.
10. Children take everything for granted.

God alone is our true treasure. Only He can satisfy the human heart.

Many people think that the greatest thing they can devote their lives to is the accumulation of money and possessions.

Others think the greatest thing they can do is to satisfy every selfish whim and desire, and to indulge every passion, instinct, and appetite.

Still others think that all they need to do is to have as much fun as they can for as long as they can.

Some think that to have their name in newspaper headlines, to be conspicuous and popular is what they want more than anything else.

Thank God for those who are convinced that the highest use of life lies in other goals and in a different direction.

If I had only one question to put to you, it would be this: Does it matter? Is your faith in God such an important factor that it would matter to you to lose it? Would it make any difference?

For some of you it might not make much difference because your faith is not the kind of asset it should be. It is not all that important.

But someday if your faith were threatened with extinction, you would be on your feet in a moment, crying, "But leave that! Take some of these lesser things, but please leave me my faith!"

The invitation of Jesus is not to a dull, dreary kind of duty. It is a gift, a privilege, a feast that never goes sour. If we never catch that meaning we will continue to look for our enjoyment in the cheap, tangible things of life and turn away from the intangibles.

If a person is interested in God, he will sell all his fields and buy the field with the hidden treasure in it. He will sell all his pearls and buy the Pearl of great price. He will leave the pursuit of ordinary goals for the prize of eternal life.

The four gospels enshrine the sublime utterances of the Savior, relate intimate facts of His daily life, and reveal God's will in language that lives in the minds and hearts of men.

Penned by men from ordinary walks of life, they stand unparalleled for beauty of expression. Limited to a hand-to-hand circulation at the time they were written, they are now published in all the languages and almost all the dialects of the earth.

Dr. William Barclay wrote, "Christianity in its beginnings was like a little island of purity, surrounded on every side by a sea of paganism and impurity."

We look back upon those people and marvel that they had so little which we believe necessary for happiness. There were so many things to spell defeat and failure.

Man is fearfully and wonderfully made. The most complex machine ever devised by human hands appears as a child's toy in comparison to the human body, self repairing and self reproducing.

Man is a walking argument for God's existence, a moving advertisement of God's power, and an articulate herald of God's intelligence.

We have 25 trillion red blood corpuscles and 4 billion white corpuscles, and each is a living unit of marvelous complexity.

Where will you be when you get where you're going? Perhaps the greatest mystery is the enigma of life. We can only say we have life and that we lose it, but the life we lay down here goes on somewhere, somehow.

At what point, where and when, our personalities entered the stream of eternal existence, we do not remember.

We do know that we are born with two attributes: existence and opportunity. These are the raw materials out of which we are to make a worthwhile life.

Life is not what you find it to be; it's what you create out of your situation.

Most people lead lives, if not of quiet desperation, at least of desperate quietness.

We are made for greatness. God has given each of us all the equipment necessary to become genuinely important. You are important. God made you for greatness. Go after it!

There is a vast disproportion between the magnificent possibilities of man's inventions and the cheap, trivial, immoral uses to which we often put them. God gave us bricks to build a marvelous superstructure. Out of them we have made this Babylon.

Sooner or later we have to face the uncomfortable truth that the greatest barrier to enjoying God's best for us, to the growing of a Christ-like character, to the vitalizing of a dynamic church, to the making of a new world is man's stubborn trust in himself and his own efforts. This is the last thing even a religious person is prepared to give up and let God be Lord.

The aim of every true Christian ought to be an all-absorbing desire to be like Christ. It ought to be so strong that we would think nothing else mattered.

In the ups and downs of fortune, whether our friends are loyal or not, whether we're understood or misunderstood, these concerns, important as they are, are not the real issue. The real goal and meaning of all our achievements is that we may be more like Jesus.

Some cannot be happy at present because they have their eyes and hopes fixed on the far-distant future. So the present is a time to be lived through or endured until certain things happen.

Some parents just can't wait until their children are grown, out of school, and off their hands.

Some young people are just waiting until they are old enough to get married and settled in a home of their own.

Some business men can't be happy in the present; they are waiting until they get all their bills paid.

Some professionals and day laborers toil year after year in endless drudgery, waiting for retirement when they can be happy.

No man lives unto himself. For better or worse, for richer or poorer, in sickness and in health, till death do us part, the human family is tied together and all of us are one in need, in nature, and in destiny. Together we rise; together we fall.

Some years ago, when scholars wanted the finest sentence ever written as the epitome of the relation of religion to the thoughts of men, they asked the president of our oldest university, Harvard, to go through all the literature of all the ages to find that best sentence. He found it in the Bible.

It was written by a man named Micah in the eighth century before Christ. It will last as long as time shall last and the stars grow weary with their shining. "What doth the Lord require of thee, but to do justly, and to love mercy, and to walk humbly with thy God?" (Micah 6:8b).

The basis of prayer is the simple fact that God listens to our prayers. He wants us to bring our needs to Him. He always listens and He is more ready to hear than we are to pray.

Prayer must be in accordance with God's will. Jesus said to pray, "Thy will be done," not "Thy will be changed." We must be obedient, remain in Christ, and pray in His name.

Prayer must be sincere, never half-hearted. The closer we live to Christ, the more nearly we will pray aright, and the more we pray aright, the greater the answers to our prayers.

In prayer, we ask God what He wants rather than telling Him what we want.

In the story of Robinson Crusoe, when Crusoe was trying to tell his man, Friday, some things about the Christian faith, he came to the doctrine of the devil, who was God's enemy, using every art in trying to defeat the Kingdom of Christ in the world.

Friday asked, "Isn't God as strong as the devil?"

Crusoe answered, "Yes."

"But," asked Friday, "why God no kill the devil, so make him no more do wicked?"

Crusoe was hard pressed to find an answer. To gain time, he pretended not to have heard the question. He asked Friday what he said, hoping Friday had forgot.

No such luck.

Friday repeated, "But why not kill the devil now, not kill a great time sometime?"

That is a question we have all wanted to ask. Why does God tolerate the devil? Why doesn't God destroy him right away?

One answer that Robinson Crusoe could have given is that God does not destroy Satan now any more than He destroys you and me now. As a created being, Satan has the power of choice, the gift of free will. And he wills to do evil in the most destructive way he can.

One of the fine equestrian statues in Washington is that of Francis Asbury seated on a slow-moving horse. The pioneer preacher is meditating on some statement he has found in the

Bible, and he has his finger between the pages to mark the place at which he was reading. His tired horse has lowered his head to snap at a pestering fly on its knee.

Asbury was only a poor Methodist circuit rider. It took him a long time to get where he was going. Today a preacher gets into his high-powered automobile and he is off, madly racing down the highway to get somewhere. The important thing is not how he gets there, but what he says when he arrives.

We are living in a wonderful age. We have made progress scientifically speaking, but what are we doing spiritually? St. Paul made tents, traveled by foot for the most part across Asia and Europe as a herald of the Lord Jesus Christ. He had little money and slow means of conveyance.

With all of our transportation miracles today, surely we should be making a greater impact for the cause of Christ.

Rev. Robert Goodrich, of Dallas, tells the story of a young lady who came to see him. She was troubled and fearful about almost every aspect of living.

The pastor called in a doctor friend, who came to talk with her. After almost an hour of questions, the doctor said, "Now, young lady, there are several things I want you to do."

He named one, two, three. Then he said, "Fourth, and most important of all, I want you to always remember that life is very much like a wheel. It's going round and round, faster and faster and we find it more and more difficult to stay on. The force of its movement tends to throw us off.

"Every day some of us do slip off this wheel of sanity and have to be given a sheltered place to live for a while. All the while the wheel moves faster and faster and each of us struggles to stay on it.

"I want you to remember that at the center of this wheel is our Christian faith. Like a magnet it tends to hold us on the wheel. All the other forces may be trying to throw you off, but here at the center is your faith. Never forget that!"

The Psalms are the outpouring of the spirit of devotion to God. They are full of expressions of love and trust in God at all times. And they contain glowing testimony to the perfection of God, His love, His power, His faithfulness, and His righteousness.

They show us the human heart before God in all its moods and emotions. One can always find something in the Psalms that is in sympathy with his own spiritual state.

In all of man's experience upon the earth he has known no richer music and few deeper mysteries than the singing of birds. A Hebrew poet wrote, "The time of the singing of birds has come" (Eccl.2:12). As Jesus tried to reveal to His followers the goodness and providence of God, He pointed skyward and said, "Behold . . ."

What endears the birds to us? It is the songs they sing. There is an ageless fascination and inspiration in their songs. We loved to hear them when we were young, and we love them more as we grow older.

But why do birds sing? I asked a charming little lady, about ten years old, that question.

She answered without hesitation, "They sing because they're happy, of course!"

But why are they happy? Because they know a fourfold secret.

1. They sing because, like the human heart, they were created to sing for joy.
2. They sing because they are in love with life. Like humans they have their troubles, their pains and tragedies, but unlike men and women, they do not ruin their lives in feverish anxiety. They take the days as they come, and, in some wonderful way, they make the most of them.

    They don't stay awake at night worrying about things that ultimately do not matter. They don't spend time

worrying about what they will eat or wear the next day. They feel the joy of life intensely, as the first man must have felt in Eden.
3. They sing at their best when they are in love. Music, real music, is a part of the language of romance.
4. They sing because they have wings. We too have wings! We have wings that can lift us and save us from life's cruelest and most devastating storms.

Birds have two wings; we have at least four: Faith, Hope, Love, and Prayer.

The next time you hear a bird singing, ask God to give you a song.

CHAPTER 2

Sample Sermons from the Past

Recently a retired minister said to me, "Preachers don't preach like they used to." I'm well aware of that.

For better or for worse, preachers change, congregations change, situations change, even the language of the Bible changes.

Undoubtedly the greatest soul winner of the twentieth century—and perhaps of all time—has not changed his method, giving an invitation after his sermon; his music, "Just as I Am;" and his message, "The Bible says."

When faced with conditions similar to ours today, the Prophet Jeremiah proclaimed: "This is what the Lord says: 'Stand at the crossroads and look; ask for the ancient paths, ask where the good way is, and walk in it, and you will find rest for your souls.'"(6:16).

God's truth and human nature never change. The Bread of Life never becomes stale. The following sermons should help us to recapture some of the flavor of the past.

What Is God Saying to Us Today?

"God, who at sundry times and in divers manners spake in time past unto the fathers by the prophets, Hath in these last days spoken unto us by his Son, whom he hath appointed heir of all things, by whom, also he made the worlds" (Heb.1:1-2).

It is the nature of God to reveal Himself. The idea of a God who speaks His mind is a fascinating subject around which the minds of men have revolved for centuries. How does God communicate to men His mind, His nature, and His will? It is the clear conviction of New Testament writers that God has given to man a clear revelation of Himself. They don't say that it began with Jesus, nor that it will end with Him.

Phillips Brooks said, "God is always teaching you just as much truth as you can learn. From the beginning He has hovered about man's mind with an unbroken Presence. Whenever there was any opening, He has thrust in some knowledge of Himself—and He limits the revelation of Himself by nothing but the capacity of every man to take in and hold His revelation."

God reveals Himself in various ways.

I. Creation. From the beginning of time, God has been revealing His nature through the nature of creation.

The Apostle Paul said that even the most unenlightened are without excuse for not knowing something of God's mind because that which may be known of Him is all about us, clearly seen in all the things that are made.

When we are asked to believe that the world and all that is in it came about by chance or by a series of accidents over millions of years, our common sense revolts. That "chance theory" doesn't make sense.

When I look at a house, I know a carpenter built it. When I look at my watch, I know a jeweler made it. When I log onto my computer, I marvel at the skill required to produce it. But never has a carpenter, jeweler, or craftsman so well expressed his creative mind as God speaks His in the wonderful works of creation. Creation is an eloquent word spoken by the living God. It reveals a God who loves beauty, order, mystery and power.

II. The Bible. God speaks His mind and reveals His nature through the pages of the Bible.

Some people are disappointed to discover that the Bible is not a textbook with chapters—one, two, three explaining God—that it does not put down in simple language who God is and what He is like. But the Bible is not a magic Book. It is a revelation of a just and holy God and the story of how men in some measure learned of God's will, His power, and His love. If we take out of the world the Bible and its effect upon humanity, we won't have enough left for a decent rummage sale.

What we find in the Bible is not a meaningless jumble of events without pattern or purpose. It is rather the unfolding of a righteous will and the living expression of a Person, the Lord Jesus Christ, The Living Word, made flesh and dwelling among us to lead us to God.

III. The Word made Flesh. Here is the mind and heart and nature of the living God brought near to us, spelled out in the language of a life. There has never been anyone like Him on this earth. For more than twenty centuries, men have been looking at that life with microscopic scrutiny and have yet to find one flaw, one unworthy thought or action.

The perfect revelation has been made. "In Him was life, and that life was the light of men" (John 1:4).

God is hard to know, life is hard to face, sin is hard to overcome, but Christ offers a way to God, forgiveness for sin, and power to live victoriously. Thank God for this revelation.

The Crowning Work of God's Creation

> "What is man that thou art mindful of him? and the son of man that thou visiteth him? For thou hast made him a little lower than the angels, and hast crowned him with glory and honour" (Psa.8:4-5).

One fact clearly taught in the Bible is the dignity of man, the infinite worth of the human soul. It is the underlying assumption of both the Old Testament and the New. It is found on every page of the New Testament.

Say, if you will, that the idea was borrowed from an ancient Hebrew Psalm composed by a simple-hearted shepherd who, watching his flock by night, looked up into the grandeur of the eastern sky and burst into a song of praise. Nevertheless, it sets forth an estimate of man, his place in the purpose of God, his dignity and destiny.

What is man? The Scriptures tell us that he is a person created in the image of God and crowned with glory and honor, the supreme concern of God, the only worthwhile value in the entire universe.

Like the Psalmist David, when we consider the heavens, we too ask "what is man?"

Astronomers say man is relatively insignificant. The philosophies and political ideologies classify man as nothing but a number, a pawn on a chessboard to be moved around at will.

When we consider man's own history—his endless wars, his perversities and cruelties, his stupidity—we may ask "Where is the evidence to verify the poet's rapture?"

Yet we must lay hold of this fact again and again to keep our sanity.

I. Man is made in the image of God in the intricate construction of man's being. This creature, standing halfway between an atom and a star, is the most ingenious piece of mechanism ever put together. Wherever we begin, with his hands or eyes or brain, or the inner realm of personality, we are confronted with a tangled maze of mystery and a masterpiece of engineering skill. No instrument man has ever invented can match the instrument he is!

He makes a computer or other means of communication and stands gaping in wonder at the intricacy his hand has wrought. Yet he walks about with a computer in his own head infinitely more complicated. His invention is a clumsy device in comparison with the two and a half pound brain that conceived it.

II. Man is made in the likeness of God. He cannot be lost in the animal world for he towers above it. Man begins where the animal stops. Chesterton said, "You never have to dig very deep to find the record of a man drawing a picture of a monkey, but no one yet has dug deep enough to find the record of a monkey drawing a picture of a man."

The fact that he can initiate more devilment than the animals and that he sometimes sinks to lower levels does not disprove his superiority, but rather confirms it. Animals living by instinct are quite content, but when a man tries it, he is in for trouble.

What makes man unique is not the fact that he was created by the hand of God. All things were created by God. It consists in the fact that he was created in the image of God. Thus, he can think God's thoughts, feel His presence, know His will, and receive Divine revelation.

Man is a restless child of earth—a child of eternity too; a curious mixture of dust and deity, crowned by his Creator with glory and honor and made a little less than divine. Surely God had some high purpose when He made the body, the mind, and the spirit of man.

This divine confidence in human souls should be a tremendous encouragement. How can a person assume a low self-image, stoop to anything that might deface the Divine image, or look with contempt on any person fashioned in God's image?

The Word of God in Living Language

> "And the Word was made flesh, and dwelt among us, (and we beheld his glory, the glory as of the only begotten Son the Father,) full of grace and truth" (John 1:1).

We live in a universe of which the ancient orator, with glorious imagination, said, "In the great primeval void and nothingness, God spoke!" Into absolute, eternal, timeless silence came the Word, and things began to happen.

Consider the Word made flesh, the incarnation. Who can begin to understand a mystery such as this? It would be too easy if we could grasp it. Yet the writer of this fourth Gospel, in the Prologue, writes, "And the Word was made flesh"—hands, feet, head, heart—"and dwelt among us." The Word made flesh. This is the gospel.

I. The Word of God experienced.

To be alive the Word must first of all be experienced. Just as Jesus Christ once lived on earth, so the Word of God, the Bible, lives today. It speaks with a very authentic note when it enters into our experience and becomes bone of our bone and flesh of our flesh.

We have all had the experience of reading the Bible, re-reading it, and then all of a sudden finding it come alive. Why? Because somehow it has spoken. It is no longer simply the dead, cold tracing of black pigment on white parchment. It is a vibrant, inspiring, living fact of our experience.

Jacqueline Cochran, the flyer, has written a book entitled *Stars at Noon*. In this book she gives a good illustration of this experience. She has flown the stratosphere, up and up, in the finest planes of our day. She says, "Earth-bound souls live only on the under side of the earth's atmosphere. But go up higher, above the dust and water vapor, and the sky beneath you and the earth turns dark, and you can see the stars at noon." This woman has been able to catch a vision rising above the dust and smoke that besets our earthly life, where somehow above it all there shines the bright light of reality.

The Word is first experienced, and then it has an authority, authenticity, and a vitality which expresses itself through our lives.

II. The Word must be expounded. It must be explained, its background clarified, and the various shades of meaning it contains expounded. We do that through our churches. Not only the preacher, but the layman as well is required to expound the Word.

The Apostle Paul shows us how to expound the Word by witnessing to what Christ has done for us.

III. The Word must be exemplified. The Word must be experienced; it must be expounded; but above all else, it must be exemplified.

We must practice it. We must put it to work so well in our lives that its pattern of living, its strength of impact, and its demands become apparent in our behavior. To exemplify means to give an example of, to take the precept and give it life in action.

Thousands of Christians today are languishing instead of flourishing because they are neglecting the Bible. To rightly experience, expound, and exemplify the Word demands that we read it, cherish it, and live by its teachings. The Word of God is the only sure guide through a confused world where men so generally seem to have lost their way.

Man's Response to God's Revelation

> "Here am I; send me" (Isaiah 6:8). "What wilt thou have me to do?" (Acts 9:6).

The Shorter Catechism teaches that the chief end of man is to glorify God and to enjoy Him forever. If this goal is to be attained, man must know God, understand His revelation, and know how to respond to that revelation. Man's response to God's revelation can be summed up in one word: *Worship*. If man has no desire to worship, all the rituals we use, the hymns we sing, the Scriptures we read, and the sermons we hear are of little value.

Man must have a desire to worship, be in the spirit of worship, and cultivate the attitude of worship, for "God is a spirit: they that worship Him must worship Him in spirit and in truth" (John 4:24).

The Bible contains many good examples of worship. Of the two texts above, the first is from the Old Testament. It is Isaiah's experience in the Temple. The second is from the New Testament. It is Saul's experience on the Road to Damascus.

The experiences of these two men came about in widely different ways, but in their essential elements they were quite similar. Each came in a time of crisis.

In Isaiah's case the crisis was largely national and partly personal. The king, in whom people trusted and from whom they expected great things, had died. The nation was frustrated. The death of King Uzziah really sobered Isaiah. He went into the Temple and there he saw God.

Saul's experience was both a personal and a national crisis. It involved Saul's relationship to the Jewish religion in which he was well versed and in which he was a leader. It also involved his relationship to Jesus. He was on his way to imprison men and women who were followers of Jesus. As he went about that task, he saw Jesus. Saul's experience ended in worship.

God has revealed Himself to man in many ways:

He speaks through His creation, which tells of His wisdom and power. Man stands in reverence before the mighty works of God. Stand on the brink of the Grand Canyon, and if you have any sense of spiritual realities, you will feel that God has been there carving and painting in a masterful way. Nature is not only God's manuscript but it is also His autobiography, in which He has written many wonderful things about Himself.

God is in history. If we look carefully we find the stately steps of the Almighty guiding the affairs of men and nations.

God has revealed Himself through the Bible.

Most and best of all, God has revealed Himself through His Son, Jesus Christ. When a man finds God in Christ, that man can see God everywhere.

I. The First Response.

When a man sees God, his first response is Reverence. Upon realizing who God is—the Eternal and Almighty Creator and Preserver of all things, visible and invisible, perfect in every attribute; majestic in His holiness—man falls down in reverence before Him.

When Isaiah saw God in the Temple, high and lifted up, with His train filling the Temple, Isaiah bowed in reverence. When Saul saw God on the highway, he fell to the earth. When he realized that it was Jesus speaking to him, he bowed in reverence.

So it is today with every man when he sees God. He bows in reverence.

How sad that so many people try to ignore God or push Him to the edge of their living. They know His law but do not keep it; they know His will but do not obey it; they know His love but continue to spurn it.

When people fail to reverence God, they likewise fail to reverence His Word, His house, His holy sacraments, and the services of the church.

II. The second response when a man sees God is repentance.

Isaiah saw God. Then he looked at himself. He confessed that he was undone. When he looked about him at others, he found no comfort because he discovered that he dwelt in the midst of a people of unclean lips. He saw his own unworthiness, the horror of his sin, and the sin of his nation.

Saul saw Jesus and then looked at himself as a persecutor. He found that it was "hard to kick against the pricks." Conscious of his sin and humbled in spirit, he was directed into the city where he was told what he must do.

When a man sees God and then looks at himself, he doesn't dare stand in the presence of the holy God? The only right thing for him to do is to throw himself on the mercy of God.

III. When a man sees God then looks at himself and comes to Repentance, his next response is expressed in Redemption. He is redeemed; he finds that God is a forgiving heavenly Father who is mighty to save.

Isaiah experienced that cleansing. It was a marvelous experience. Saul had a similar experience when he entered Damascus. A transforming power came into his life. He was changed from persecutor to preacher. He got a new sense of direction and a new name. From that day forward, he was Paul, the Christian, the foremost character in the early Christian church.

IV. When a man sees God, becomes conscious of his sin, and experiences forgiveness, he will desire to render acceptable service. This is the natural and immediate result of such an experience.

Isaiah heard a voice calling, "Whom shall I send, and who will go for us?" His answer was, "Here am I; send me." God did send him to a difficult task. Isaiah went, was faithful in the performance of the task, and met with good success. If Isaiah had kept out of politics, he would never have appeared in the Old Testament.

Paul made a similar response. Afterward he said, "I was not disobedient unto the heavenly vision." His task was not easy. It led among hostile people, to intense suffering for the cause of Christ. But through his abundant labors a great company of people were brought to the Master.

So it is with the person who experiences God today. He will hear the voice of God. The answer can be "Here am I; send me" or "What wilt thou have me to do?" God will not only have something for him to do, but He will help him to do it.

The Resurrection

There is enough tragedy in the New Testament to make it the saddest book ever written. Yet it is the most joyful book in the world. It opens with the birth of Jesus and ends with a great multitude which no man can number singing Hallelujah choruses around the great white throne of God. No matter where you open it, you always hear a note of joy.

The central theme of the apostolic teaching is bound up with the belief, not that Jesus survived spiritually, but that He was raised from the dead. There are other important subjects, but none so important as this one.

St. Paul said, "If Christ be not risen, then is our preaching vain, and your faith is vain" (I Cor.15:14). If Christ is not risen, this Gospel we love is a fake. It is worth no more than Buddhism, Theosophy, Christian Science, or Hinduism.

Renan, in his story of Jesus, pictured Him hanging on the cross, with drooping head, matted hair, and pale, blood-streaked face. Storm clouds covered the sky, and black-pinioned birds were flying through the gloom. Everything about the scene spelled defeat. At the end, he put the word, "Finis."

Jesus did die that way. But He didn't have to. One word from His lips and all the forces of heaven would have rushed to His rescue.

Yes, it was finished. What was finished? The plan of salvation!

But the world was not finished with Jesus. They laid Him in the tomb and they said, "We'll seal it and put a Roman guard around it because He said He would rise, and we will show the world that He was a fake."

When Paul preached the resurrection to those old philosophers at Athens, they called him a babbler and "a setter forth of strange doctrines." But Paul said, "Why should it be thought a thing incredible that God should raise the dead?" Admit God, and all doubts will vanish into thin air.

Do you expect to limit the God who, out of nothing created the heavens and the earth? The God who made the inanimate animate and called into being every living thing? The Author of life itself? If He couldn't do it, we haven't any God at all.

The resurrection of Jesus cannot be called into question any more than the historical certainty of the assassination of Julius Caesar.

I. Some try to explain away His appearances.

   A. An angel at the tomb said, "He is risen."
   B. The disciples said He arose. If they lied about it, isn't it strange that they would die for what they knew was a lie.

   Why do we have the account of a weak woman offering to carry away the body of a full-grown man?

   Why did they make Christ fold the napkin so carefully? The disciples who entered the tomb were very much impressed by the way the grave cloths which bound Christ's body had just collapsed as if the body had evaporated.
   C. Jesus appeared 11 times after the resurrection.
   D. His enemies have never been able to present one iota of evidence that He did not rise.

   The Apostles went up and down the land preaching this doctrine everywhere. Those who chose not to believe it could only say that the disciples stole His body.
   E. They all have to admit that the grave was empty. If it was empty, and there was no resurrection, either His friends or His foes took the body away.
   F. Of course if His enemies took it away, they could have produced the body and stopped the mouths of the disciples.

II. Some say that Jesus never died; He was just in a swoon. The cool air of the tomb and the odor of the spices revived Him, and He got up and left the tomb.

   One historian put it right when he said that a man who crept forth half-dead from the grave and crawled about, a fit subject for a hospital, could have never impressed His disciples that He was the conqueror of death.

   Could a person suffering from five terrible wounds, all of them involving serious loss of blood, lie in a cold grave for 36 hours and then coming out of a coma, push away a heavy stone that had been rolled in front of the entrance, and not only stagger out of the tomb, but remove the grave cloths, procure other clothing, evade the 16 guards, and persuade His followers that He had conquered death?

Had His own followers believed He would rise from the dead, they would have been waiting around the tomb for Him. Instead they were shut up in a room in Jerusalem, with doors barred for fear.

The greatest proof is the immediate change in their attitude.

III. Some have said that the disciples had a brain-storm, an hallucination; they just thought they saw Him.

This is called the Vision Theory. You can prove how absurd it is in a dozen ways.

A. If it were only a vision, how did it happen, at times, to last so long? Visions are over in a few minutes at most. But the walk to Emmaus lasted for hours.
B. Jesus appeared to all eleven disciples at the same time. On one occasion 500 people saw him. Who ever heard of this many people having the same vision at the same time? Deny one miracle, and you have to substitute 500 in its place.
C. If they were just visions, why did they end so suddenly? At the end of 40 days they stopped.

   Mrs. Eddy said that He didn't rise because He didn't die, but was alive in the tomb demonstrating Christian Science. I suppose that's what she is doing now.
D. In spite of what Jesus said about His resurrection, His followers were not expecting Him to rise. When they did find the tomb empty, they thought someone had taken His body away. When the disciples were told He had risen, they didn't believe it.

Finally, when Jesus did appear, instead of seeing the fulfillment of His word, "they were terrified and affrighted, and supposed they had seen a spirit."

The two disciples going to Emmaus after hearing about the resurrection, told Jesus what had happened, but they had no idea what had become of Jesus.

God raised Him from the dead to make good the word of His Son and to establish beyond all doubt the truth of His divinity.

He did it so that all who are united to Jesus Christ by faith may know that they, too, will be raised from the dead.

He did it to furnish every believer the solid assurance that he is justified in Christ Jesus.

When the cross was lifted on Golgotha there was not one Christian in the world. Then came the miracle of the resurrection, and suddenly His own people saw Who He really was. The resurrection was God's Amen to the tremendous claims Christ had made.

Thomas Discovered What Job Sought

> There are two verses I will use together: "Oh, that I knew where I might find Him" (Job 23:3) and "Thomas answered and said unto Him, my Lord and my God!" (John 20:28).

Job, the sufferer, was not an atheist. He believed in the existence of God, but his trouble was how to locate Him. In the loneliness of his soul and in the agony of his sufferings, this cry, "Oh, that I knew where I might find Him," was born. To discover God—to be sure of Him, to be in fellowship with Him—is the greatest discovery anyone can make.

What is it that drives man forward in his quest for God? This longing of which people of every age throughout the world have been so conscious where does it come from? Have people who profess to have found God merely been playing a game of "let's pretend," out of which they wrangled some kind of peace, but which, in reality, is nothing more than a pathological fantasy?

It is clear that Job regarded God as the greatest need of his life. Here we discern a depth of longing unsurpassed in the Bible.

He felt that if he could be sure of God, if only he could have a sense of His presence, he could endure anything!

Are you sure of God, not merely in an intellectual way, but because you are in fellowship with Him?

Surely there must be something behind the religious longings of mankind and the religious experiences of the human family. God has created us for Himself and we can find no rest until we rest in Him. The longing for God exists within every human breast, as John Calvin said, "A sense of deity is inscribed on every heart." God has so made us that it cannot be eradicated. Job utters that universal, anguished cry: "Oh, that I knew where I might find Him!"

It must be a fearful thing to go down to the loneliness of the grave without God; to witness the break-up of the mortal frame; to be obliged to face the grim reality that the sands of time are fast running out, and not be able to say, "Yea, though I walk through the valley of the shadow of death, I will fear no evil: for thou art with me."

But that need not be. In reality God is always near. He reigns and controls the destinies of men and nations. He is on the throne.

The story of Thomas' great discovery is so well known that it need not be repeated. Thomas, the most-unjustly-dealt-with of the apostles, was present at the Lord's second appearance after the resurrection. He was determined to see and feel the scars to make sure that Jesus was, indeed, his Lord and Master.

Touching was not necessary. Thomas did see. Falling in adoring worship at Jesus' feet, he cried, "My Lord and my God!" Thomas had found his God in a risen Christ.

On one occasion Philip said, "Lord, show us the Father, and it sufficeth us." Jesus replied, "He that hath seen me hath seen the Father." Jesus was, in the days of His flesh, and still is, "Immanuel—God with us." It is possible to find God up to a point, and within certain limits, apart from Christ. Job and other patriarchs found Him. But to find Him in His fullness, in the completeness of His nature, His love, and His power, we must find Him in Christ just as Thomas did.

The New Testament brings God to us in Christ through the miracles; the sayings of Jesus; His compassion; His understanding; His love for little children; His rebuke of the Phariseees for their hollowness and hypocrasy; His abhorrence of sin and refusal to compromise with it; His reaction to the hatred, injustices, and revilings of His enemies: His life and His ignominious death.

The character of Jesus Christ towers over all humanity, sublime beyond all powers of description. Jesus was the answer to Job's cry. He is the answer to your cry too.

What are the results of this discovery of God? In the case of Thomas, three results are evident:

I. The first result is devotion.

Thomas fell in worship at the feet of Jesus, for in Him he had discovered God. Archbishop William Temple wrote, "To worship is to quicken the conscience by the holiness of God, to feed the mind with the truth about God, to open the heart to the love of God, to purge the imagination by the beauty of God, and to devote the will to the purpose of God."

II. The second result of Thomas' discovery was dedication.

In that moment Jesus passed from the circumference of Thomas' life to the very center. Life, for this man previously plagued and tortured by doubts, had no purpose. He was drifting before, but now he had found a safe anchorage.

Tradition says that Thomas later went to India where his preaching and witness for the risen Christ were greatly blessed.

III. The third effect of Thomas' discovery was deliverance.

Doubts and fears, anxieties and mysteries vanished in this moment of his experience. He faced the future with confidence and with purpose.

Thus Thomas discovered what Job sought many centuries earlier. Multitudes have made a similar discovery. They have proved that God is knowable in Christ, that personal communion with the Lord is possible today. It has been the secret of both their strength and their service.

We could well write over the entire Old Testament the words of Job 23:3 "O that I knew where I might find Him." It is a book of unsatisfied longings.

Then we could write over the New Testament, "We have found Him."

Pentecost Today

Some of the last words of our blessed Lord before His ascension into heaven were: "But ye shall receive power, after that the Holy Ghost is come upon you . . ." (Acts 1:8a).

I. The Promise

    A. Here is a promise of power.
        He knew His followers needed power.
    B. It is a promise fulfilled at Pentecost.
        In obedience to their Master's command to tarry in Jerusalem, they waited patiently, persistently, purposefully, and prayerfully. They did not wait in vain.
    C. This promise is for God's children today.
        It is not a promise for the disciples exclusively, or for the saints of the early church only; it is for every believer in Christ Jesus.

II. The Purpose

"And ye shall be witnesses unto me" Acts 1:8a). God does not give the fullness of the Spirit for selfish reasons. Pentecost means power to witness by life as well as by lip. Thus the Spirit-filled person receives the necessary power.

    A. Power to Live Victoriously
        As you read the New Testament you will soon be

convinced that the Christian life is one of victory over the world, the flesh, and the devil; a life of joy and purity; and one of soul-winning capability.

B. Power to Love Fervently

One of the historians of the first century commented on the love of those early Christians: "Behold how these Christians love one another." John says, "We know that we have passed from death unto life, because we love the brethren" (I John 3:14a).

C. Power to Pray Effectively

James says, "The effectual fervent prayer of a righteous man availeth much" (5:16b). This was certainly true of the early Christians who had to face trouble, endure great trials, and suffer intense persecution, even martyrdom. They proved again and again that effectual, fervent prayer avails much.

D. Power to Study Diligently

The disciples learned more within three days of Pentecost than they learned in three years sitting at the feet of Jesus. Why? Because Jesus was *with* them; the Holy Spirit was *in* them.

E. Power to Testify Courageously

"And when they had prayed, the place was shaken where they were assembled together; and they were all filled with the Holy Ghost and spake the word of God with boldness" (Acts 4:31).

Some three thousand people were added to their number that day (Acts 2:41b). This is how the early church grew. In his commentary on the book of Acts, J.B. Phillips says, "they went everywhere preaching the Word and within one generation that rotten, sodden Empire of Rome was shaken to its very foundation."

F. Power to Give Generously

From the beginning, Christians were urged to give to the less fortunate among them. Early followers of Jesus often lost their possessions and their jobs, especially during the days when Rome required everyone to burn a pinch of incense and proclaim Caesar as Lord. Those who had earthly possessions gladly shared with those who did not.

Christians today give generously to worthy causes, especially to help the poor and spread the gospel.

G. Power to Suffer Uncomplainingly

Stephen, the first Christian martyr we read about, even prayed as Jesus did for God to forgive his tormentors.

Paul and Silas sang in the midst of their persecution. Their song led to the conversion of their jailer and his household.

Christians around the world still suffer intense persecution, even martyrdom, for the faith.

III. The Place

Where were these Spirit-filled Christians to witness? " . . . in Jerusalem, and in all Judea, and in Samaria, and unto the uttermost part of the earth" (Acts 1:8b).

Pentecost means a church on fire! Pentecost means a witnessing church! Pentecost means a church that sends missionaries all over the world.

Acts: The Gospel of the Holy Spirit

The Book of Acts has been called the Gospel of the Holy Spirit. It is impossible to read this exciting book without being profoundly stirred and even disturbed. Stirred because here we see Christianity in action for the first time; yet we cannot help feeling disturbed as we are moved. For this surely reveals the church as it was meant to be. It is vigorous and invincible, for these are the days before it became fat and short of breath through prosperity or muscle-bound by over-organization.

No one can read this book without being convinced that there is Someone here at work besides mere human beings. It is a matter of record that never before has any small body of ordinary people so moved the world that their outraged enemies could say that these men "have turned the world upside down."

On the pages of this book the fresh air of heaven is blowing. This is the beginning of the Christian era.

The period covered by this book is from the Ascension of Christ to Paul's imprisonment in Rome—about 33 years. Luke is the author. It is an interesting guess that Luke intended to write a third book, for the present books ends on a triumphant, but rather unfinished note. If so, he was never able to complete the story. No one knows why.

It is easy to think of this period of the church's history as an enthusiastic time of adolescence, followed by our now well-disciplined period of maturity, but that makes it too easy. We have unquestionably lost something.

Something very powerful and unusual is happening here on every page of the Book of Acts.

The Day of Pentecost is called the birthday of the Christian church, for on that day the Holy Spirit came to believers in a very special way. And the church grew.

The second chapter of Acts speaks of addition—"the Lord added . . . ." The rest of the book speaks of multiplication: Acts 4:32; 6:2; 8:7; 9:31.

The church continued where Jesus left off. The emphasis is on "this Jesus." In Acts 2 it is used seven times.

The three prominent ideas of Acts are (1) Jesus is alive; (2) He has come through the Holy Spirit to abide forever; and (3) He *is*—not *will be*—Lord.

The early church in the Book of Acts was the most nearly free from fear of any society before or since. In the Gospels Jesus exhorted His followers "fear not." In Acts we see a people who were not afraid. The more they were threatened, the more they testified to their faith in Jesus. They knew that Christ in them could transform every situation, solve every problem, and turn every opposition into an opportunity.

Three things characterized the early Christians: (1) They were courageous, (2) They were cheerful, and (3) They were always getting into trouble.

It is perhaps unfortunate that we so often speak of the events at Pentecost as the coming of the Holy Spirit as though He came into existence at that time. The Spirit had existed previously and moved upon men throughout the Old Testament. But after Pentecost the Holy Spirit became the dominant reality and power in the life of the church.

1. The Holy Spirit was the source of divine guidance.
2. All the leaders of the church were men of the Spirit. It was a Spirit-filled church. There are more than forty references to the Holy Spirit in the first thirteen chapters of Acts.
3. The Spirit was the source of day-to-day courage and power.
4. The measure of the Spirit which a man can possess is conditioned by the kind of man he is. God does not give His power to a sinful person.

Victorious Living

> "Now unto Him that is able to keep you from falling, and to present you faultless before the presence of His glory with exceeding great joy . . ." (Jude 24:25).

He is able to keep you from falling! He is able to present you faultless before the throne!

Dr. E. Stanley Jones says, "Heal me at the heart, then let the world come on!"

Two men go into the slums of a great city. One is a self-indulgent, worldly sinner; the other is a sincere Christian. One comes out worse because the evil of his own heart responded to the evil of his environment. The other comes out a better man because he not only has resisted temptation, but he has also brought an elevating influence to all those he met.

I. The first element of victorious living is a sanctified heart, a heart that has been cleansed from inner contradictions.

Resisting the uprisings of carnality usually ends in defeat. How much better it is to get rid of the "old man" and put on the "new man!" Then you have not only outward consistency, but an inward calm as well. A man might keep a box of rattlesnakes under control by sitting on the lid, but it is much safer to kill the snakes.

II. The second element of victory is a good supply of the Christian graces. Paul calls them fruits of the Spirit: "love, joy, peace, long-suffering, gentleness, goodness, faith, meekness, temperance."

Instead of resentment, bitterness, and strife, the beauty of Christian grace is brought out by the contacts and experiences of life. Living a holy life is positive, not negative.

III. The third element of victory is a Spirit-directed and Spirit-empowered service.

No one is satisfied with uselessness. The Holy Spirit guides us into places where we can do something really worthwhile. Philip was directed by the Spirit to go down toward Gaza. There he intercepted a hungry soul who was ready to be led into salvation.

IV. The fourth element of victory is unbroken fellowship with God.

Nothing is more important for a Christian than to keep in touch with God. Disobedience and sin spoil this fellowship. Enoch is described as a man who walked with God. What a testimony!

The writer to the Romans was so conscious of this spiritual strength which comes from a Spirit-filled life that he throws out the challenge: "Who shall separate us from the love of Christ?

Shall tribulation, or distress, or persecution, or famine, or nakedness, or peril, or sword . . . ?" Nay, in all these things we are more than conquerors through Him that loved us" (Rom. 8:35, 37).

Dreams that Come True

Hidden in the gospel of our Lord are four dreams. Men before His coming had all these dreams and had longed for their fulfillment.

I. Long ago men groped after God.
   They worshipped the sun, moon, and stars. In addition, they set up altars to "The Unknown God."
   The dreamer in Ur of the Chaldees in far-off Babylon and the dreamer in the land of the Nile caught a vision of a God of yearning and of love, who was of purer eyes than to behold iniquity and who "would not that any should perish."
   That dream came true in Him who said, "He that hath seen me, hath seen the Father" and "If I be lifted up, I will draw all men unto me."

II. Another dream was the hope that somehow and somewhere there might be forgiveness for sin.
   Men have always believed that there might be some atonement for sin. They have made their children pass through the fire as a sacrifice to Moloch or thrown their babies into the river, hoping by the fruit of their loins to atone for the sins of their souls. Others have sat on a bed of spikes, walked through the fire, and sacrificed valuable possessions in their attempt to win the favor of their gods.

III. Another dream has been the dream of the future. Job asked, "If a man die, shall he live again?"
   We build a home. Then we learn too soon that we must give up that home. Someone else will move in. We're happy and strong; then our health fails. We fall in love. Then that loved one is taken and we're devastated.

Ingersoll wrote, "Whether in midsea, or among the breakers of the further shore, a wreck must at last mark the end of each and every life . . . ."
IV. There is another dream of the brotherhood of men.
Everyone who keeps up with the news these days knows that dream will never be realized in this world.

The dream of humanity—the dream of God, the Father; the dream of atonement for erring humanity; the dream of a happy heart; the dream of the fellowship of love—all are realized in our message of Jesus Christ and His kingdom.

What Kind of Persons

{This is based on a message by Dr. T. W. Willingham, on the *Showers of Blessing* Nazarene radio program, probably aired in the 1960's}

Peter has just been warning of catastrophic events. "But the day of the Lord will come as a thief in the night; in which the heavens shall pass away with a great noise, and the elements will melt with fervent heat, the earth also and the works that are therein shall be burned up" (II Peter 3:10).

He goes on to say, "Seeing then that all these things shall be dissolved, what manner of persons ought ye to be in all holy conversation and godliness" (v.11).

I. I must be certain of my own salvation.
    We will have more to answer for because we have had more light than some have had.
II. I must be alert to the possibility of backsliding.
III. I must see to it that my life is a holy life.
    There's a difference between a holiness man and a holy man.
IV. I should be mindful of the promises concerning the Second Coming of Christ and be watching for His coming.
V. I must be tied very loosely to the things of this world. Remember Lot's wife.

VI. I must be alert to opportunities to win as many souls as possible.
VII. I should be looking for a new heaven and a new earth.

The Elder Brother
(Luke 15:11-32)

If Jesus had found the Scribes and Pharisees diligently and earnestly trying to lead sinners to God, He could have made this story have a beautiful ending. It might have gone like this:

One day the elder son came in and asked his father and mother to sit down with him in the living room, for he had something important to discuss with them.

When they were comfortably seated, he said, "Mother, I heard you sobbing last night. I know you are unhappy because my younger brother is in the far country somewhere and we don't know where he is.

"The other night I came in rather late, and I noticed a light in my brother's window. I got in fast and ran up to his room. I was going to hug him and tell him I was so glad he was back, for life had been miserable around here without him. Mother, how long have you been keeping a light burning in his room?"

Then he turned to his father, "Dad, I saw you the other day. You and I don't talk about him very much, but I saw you when you went up on the hill where you could see way down the road. I knew you were watching for him. I plowed on, but the tears plowed some furrows down my dusty cheeks.

"Now, let's face it; we're miserable, all of us are. Let me go and find that boy. I can find him and bring him home!"

The mother said, "No, no, no, you can't go. We've lost one boy; we can't let you do it!"

His dad reached over, patted his shoulder, and said, "Son, you are a noble lad, but we can't let you go."

The boy got up and walked around. "Look," he said, "it's just like a funeral around here. I miss him as much as you do. I try to look happy, but all the time I'm crying on the inside. I've got to go and find my brother!"

The next morning he starts out.

Then one day the father was out on the little hill where he could see down the road. There he saw two boys coming up that dusty lane. He couldn't get there fast enough. No doubt he went to that youngest son first, smothered his made-up speech against his shoulder and put new clothes on him.

Then he turned to the older brother and whispered, "All that I have is yours. You're the finest son I ever knew."

The father ordered a servant to kill two of those fat calves and call the neighbors in to celebrate.

The place of honor would belong to the elder son tonight. He's the hero of the story.

Life, an Opportunity for Spiritual Adventure

The best and greatest use of life is this: An opportunity for spiritual adventure and discovery. That means to welcome life, to be grateful for it, and to use it as an opportunity day by day to discover more about God. The Christian life can be described as getting to know God better every day.

I. Life is monotonous and dull for most people. Each day is a weary repetition of yesterday. Tomorrow? It holds nothing more than the same dull round of activities.

But for the one who is alive to his world and wants to keep on being alive, the mystery of life, of what is coming next, or what might possibly happen tomorrow prevents life from becoming routine. SOMETHING WONDERFUL and DIFFERENT might happen!

II. The danger facing all of us is not that we will make an absolute failure of life, nor that we will go out into outright sinful acts, nor that we will get to the place where we feel that life has no meaning, and we'll go out and end it.

The danger is that we will miss its deepest and most abiding happiness, unconscious of the presence of God, and be content to have it so.

The complexity of life is stealing something from us that we can ill afford to lose.

The person who wants to know the full richness of life, who covets knowledge of its secrets, and who would live it to the utmost must accept the gift of life as an opportunity for spiritual adventure. Life is an adventure or it isn't much at all.

III. Life must always be regarded as an adventure with risks on every hand. Our lives swing between risks and opportunities.
IV. Life is an unending exchange of material we can't keep for riches we cannot lose. To be rich and rewarding, life must be lived with a vision, a dream that gives life its meaning, its drive, and its power.

If a man chooses to devote his life to some goal that will outlast his short span of years to help make the world a better place, he will know raptures and sorrows hidden from others. He will make discoveries hidden from other eyes. He will experience heartaches and suffering that he could have escaped. But he will find a joy and a peace that others do not share.

V. Life is not made up of a few mountain-top experiences but of daily care and toil. With God's help, however, we can make it more productive.

A. We can live affirmatively, accentuate the positive, and eliminate the negative.
B. We can live with courage and compassion and with thankful and loving hearts.
C. We can live with holiness and intensity and joy.

People will listen to those who love God and find delight in serving Him, who have joy in their religion, whose religion is not a weight, but wings.

Will He Find Faith?

" . . . When the Son of Man comes, will He find faith?" (Luke 18:8b).

Jesus was always asking questions. Some of them bother me, I must confess. Here is a question of real significance. Will He find faith on the earth?

In the light of our thinking we would probably answer as follows:

"Yes, Master, You will find millions singing praises to Your name and offering petitions before Your throne.

"You will find that mighty temples and cathedrals have been built; and You will find power, influence, and wealth in Your church.

"You will hear men reciting creeds, beautiful creeds into which have been poured the rich experiences of generations, creeds born in blood.

"You will find theologies hoary with age, splendid with diction, around which men have fought and died.

"You will find that Your religion has expressed itself in poetry, music, and art of the highest and best quality.

"You will find mighty, huge organizations moving ponderously down through the centuries, and men and women everywhere sharing the blessings that You have brought.

"You will find Your followers are educated, cultured, and highly respectable, and that we have come a long way from the time of the Apostle Paul."

But I hear Him say, "That's not what I asked you. I'm asking you 'Will I find faith?' Not some declaration of belief, some show of ecclesiastical pride, nor some huge piece of machinery. But will I find men and women walking in the way of faith?"

Will He find us with an appreciation of spiritual values?

Will He find human contacts marked by spiritual impulses?

Will He find that men have discovered their highest loyalty in Him, or at least are making an effort to discover it?

If love is to be tested, how far have we gone? If this way is to be measured by sacrifice, how far have we walked?

The greatest of sins is to know Christ, yet fail to be like Him; to see the saving power of His grace, and yet not feel it; to have before us His example as our highest ideal, yet fail to follow it.

Are you looking for a worthy challenge?

What is the ruling passion of your life?
Who is your master?
The right answers to these questions will assure that He will find faith—at least in you.

Our Glorious God
Isaiah 40

The purpose of this study is to inspire us to be aware of God always and to worship Him who is our Creator, Comforter, and Redeemer. Westminster Catechism (1614) asks, "What is the chief end of man?" Its answer is "To glorify God and enjoy Him forever."

In Isaiah 40, the prophet admonished God's people

I. To be faithful in times of distress. He wrote his eloquent words about God during the reign of Hezekiah. Hezekiah was a godly leader. But dark days faced the nation. The prophet used the word *comfort*, which means to cause to breathe again.
II. To ask God for pardon. God gets no joy out of the punishment sin brings. He delights in pardon and restoration.
III. To trust Him to guide on pleasant ways. God wants to make the road home as pleasant as possible.
   Surely the omnipotent, omniscient, immutable, inexhaustible God can be trusted to do what is best for us.
IV. To mount up with wings. That is to get above our difficulties into the clear sunshine of God's presence.

Every runner on the track or every rower in the boat knows what it is to reach the stage where he finds what he calls his "second wind." He has adjusted to the strain. He has renewed his strength.

The youths "shall faint and be weary." Whether they are Christian or not, the physical fails.

But there is a power that is greater than nature. It is the power of God's extra grace. God has made His promise to those who are weary in the journey; their strength shall be replenished.

"They shall mount up with wings as eagles." I like the sound of that. I love to think of the eagle's horizon, of his vision.

As one gets older, enthusiasm cools. The poetry will likely fade. But I love to think of our being lifted into the upper air on wings! That means difficulties surmounted, obstacles overcome. It is glorious to feel that we can rise above the sorrows and sins and cares of this earth and find a wider field of vision and hope because we serve a glorious God.

Sanctification Then and Now

> "And when the day of Pentecost was fully come...."(Acts 2:1)

The coming of the Holy Spirit on the Day of Pentecost was the answer to Jesus' prayer (John 17) that his disciples and "all who believe on me through their word" be sanctified.

Just before His ascension, our Lord gave specific instructions as to the preparation for and reception of the Sanctifier.

Fifty days later, the Holy Spirit came. Was the event God's timing, or did it take that long for the disciples to get ready? At any rate, "they were all with one accord."

What God did for those in the Upper Room that day is needed in the life of every believer. There is no difference in sanctification then and now.

I. Sanctification then and now means hearts are purified by faith.
II. Sanctification then and now means being filled with the Holy Ghost.

    A. The fullness of the Spirit produces Christlikeness.
    B. The fullness of the Spirit banishes self-seeking and selfishness.

C. The fullness of the Spirit washes out the world and worldly desires.
D. The fullness of the Spirit raises the level of love to perfect love for God and man.

III. Sanctification then and now means being endued with power.

A. Power to witness,
B. Power to resist temptation,
C. Power to accomplish the work God calls us to do,
D. Power to glorify God in daily living,
E. Power to face the pressures of life.

IV. Sanctification then and now brings harmony. On the Day of Pentecost, "they were all of one accord in one place." The major source of discord is people out of harmony with God.
V. Sanctification then and now motivates people to act for God.

Glossalalia

First, back of all I say, I consider charismatic and Pentecostal Christians my brothers and sisters in Christ. I know they are interested in the work of the Holy Spirit. I believe, however, that what is called the unknown tongue, or glossalalia, is a confusing mistake coming from misunderstanding of the Scripture. I think of it as a mistaken by-path and not the main road.

Before the present century, almost no commentary on Scriptures had the New Testament references to "other" or "unknown" tongues to refer to anything beyond what was both in the original Greek and the English King James' time. The exact meaning of the word "tongues" was "languages"—languages which were spoken and understood somewhere on earth.

The gift of languages Paul dealt with in his Corinthian letter was not the same at all as the one recorded at Pentecost. There, as I see it, the miracle was the gift of what scholars call *Xenolalia* tongue, but a well known human tongue which the speakers had not learned or used before. The miracle at Pentecost was the gift of a well known language.

There is no evidence that the apostles were aware that they were speaking in these other languages, and no evidence that they felt themselves in a mind-altering ecstasy which prompted them to speak without knowing what they were saying. As soon as the first burst of joyous witnessing had settled down, Peter rose to preach, probably in the Koine Greek, or maybe Aramaic, languages which all, or nearly all, who were present could understand.

Only in his first letter to the Corinthians (Chapter 12) does St. Paul mention the continuing ability to use other languages besides one's mother tongue as a "gift." The apostle tells them (and us) that in the community of believers, the Holy Spirit blesses, empowers, and extends each member's natural talents. He calls the resulting ability to preach, prophesy, administer, teach, heal, and speak or interpret other than one's own language "gifts of the Spirit."

The gift of languages was the power, whether by training or by miracle, called "xenolalia" to declare or interpret gospel truth in one or more human tongues besides one's own. But Paul said that a language which allows a person to speak to God only is of no value to the church.

I am going to borrow from a life-long friend, Dr. Timothy Smith. In his book *Called Unto Holiness,* He says, "The reason that this gift was so important in Corinth was that Corinth was a rapidly growing commercial city whose residents spoke many different languages. Christianity was winning more converts among the numerous ethnic subgroups in the congregation than among the native-born Greeks. Many of the converts found the Greek, spoken in Corinth and also in Christian gatherings, difficult to use. Members gifted in interpretation, therefore, were priceless. Little wonder then that a problem should have arisen from the frequent use in their meetings of languages unknown to most of those present."

Dr. Smith goes on to reconstruct what was taking place: "When new converts of non-Greek background found themselves struggling to phrase their prayers in Greek, or to express their testimonies, or celebrate their joy in that tongue, they often lapsed back into speaking their native language, not waiting for an interpreter."

A natural and loving response among the congregation was to say to a brother or sister, "I did not understand what you said, but I know the Spirit in whose power I sensed you were speaking and He teaches us all." A difference of opinion then arose as to whether an interpreter or, indeed, any spiritual gift of languages was necessary, since Jesus had promised that the Spirit would guide Christians into all truth.

In Chapter 14, Paul explained that speaking or praying in a language his hearers did not understand did not edify the church because the building up of the Christian community depended upon the daily increase of their comprehension of the gospel. Speaking in an unknown tongue without an interpreter, Paul wrote, and especially doing so without waiting upon one another by taking turns, produced confusion and reversed the work of Pentecost.

Paul also made it clear that Christians speaking in tongues know what they are saying. But he places a low premium on words that are not understandable.

It seems that usually a seeker observes speaking in tongues in others before he experiences it himself.

All of us know some people who claim their speaking in unknown tongues is an evidence of holiness. Yet their lives by no means measure up to God's standards.

C. Peter Wagner tells the story of a missionary couple in Argentina, who were having trouble with the new language. One night in a preaching service they were given the ability for a while to speak in fluent Spanish and bring a message of salvation to their people. That is the real gift of tongues.

The Divine Christ

> " . . . I am the light of the world: he that followeth me shall not walk in darkness, but shall have the light of life" (John 8:12).

Jesus was either God incarnate or the greatest egotist the world has ever known. Let's look at some of His sayings:

"Whosoever believeth in me shall be saved." He claims that He and He alone is Savior; He and He alone has the power to introduce men to God.

"I am the way; he that climbeth up some other way is a thief and a robber."

"Come unto me, all ye that labor . . . and I will give you rest."

It would be blasphemy for a mere man to say what Christ said.

He assumed power to forgive sins. " . . . the Son of Man hath power on earth to forgive sins."

The things Jesus did and the words He said are the wonder of the universe.

It would be worse than a farce for the best of men to claim what Christ claims, but He performs what He promises!

It would be strange if, being who He is, He should say less.

I. I believe in the God-hood of Jesus because of the teachings of the Bible.

   A. The Old Testament; messianic Psalms; Prophets
   B. His birth—"The Word became flesh."

     What a birth! There was no such event before, nor has there been one since. Angels sang, shepherds wondered, wise men came to worship. The virgin mother died and was buried, and God wisely hid her grave. The shepherds returned to their flocks. The wise men returned to their homes another way and dropped out of history. But Christ is still with us.

II. I believe in the God-hood of Jesus because He did things which only God could do.

   A. He worked miracles.
   B. He healed diseases.

C. He cast out devils.
D. He raised the dead.
Then there were some things He would not do.

III. I believe in His God-hood because no other man has ever been what Jesus was. If He is only human, why is He the only human to be like this?

   A. He was unmatched among men.
      1. As a man, He was hungry; as God, He fed 5,000.
      2. As a man, He was tired, slept in a boat; as God, He stilled the storm.
      3. As a man, He sat on Jacob's well; as God, He gave the water of life to a thirsty soul.
      4. As a man, He wept at the death of Lazarus; as God, He raised Lazarus from the dead.
      5. As a man, He died on a cross; as God, He rose from the grave.
      6. As a man, He led his followers to Olivet; as God He mounted up above the clouds.
      7. As a man, He walked and talked with others; as God, He loved, healed, and forgave.

   B. He would not lose sight of His far off goal. Suppose He had been satisfied to become the world's greatest teacher. He could have had wealth, power, and fame. But we could not have had salvation.
   C. He would not become discouraged enough to quit. He had not many converts, and they were mostly poor, ignorant people. His followers were few and sin was rampant.
   D. He would not accept the methods of the world.

IV. Not only did He do great things in the past, but He is still doing what no other man can do. Human nature is regenerated. He changes defeat into victory and sadness into hope.

He is either God Incarnate or He is an imposter or a lunatic. If the life that lay behind these sayings is that of a lunatic, it is a lunacy that is better than our sanity.

If Jesus is God, He can, and He will, keep His promises. All He taught is true. If Jesus is God, His cause will triumph! His cause is one of victory and the gates of hell shall not prevail against it.

The last chapters of Revelation tell us of the final outcome of God's people and the defeat of sin and evil.

"When These Things Come to Pass" Luke 21:28

When Jesus told His disciples that their magnificent Temple, the pride of every Jew, would be destroyed, these shocked men asked when and what would be the sign. Jesus listed one disastrous event after another and gave instructions as to how His followers were to react. His list includes perils similar to those we hear about on TV every night. In conclusion, He said, "And when these things begin to come to pass, then look up, and lift up your heads; for your redemption draweth nigh" (Luke 21:28).

What applied to them applies to us.

When that terrible fear is getting you by the throat and seems ready to suffocate your very soul, look up! When all the ways of life are closed against you and you can no longer see the road beneath your feet, look up! When your soul is bowed to the ground beneath the load of bitter disappointment and care that saps your strength, look up! When you just can not see any hope at all, lift up your head!

If your soul is stumbling through the gloom, reach out for the hand of the Lord! Look up and stabilize your staggering soul by a discovery of the unseen and eternal God.

You have to feel the foundations shake beneath your feet before you can sing "Rock of Ages" as it should be sung. You have to see everything falling from your grasp, and then say,

"Nothing in my hand I bring" before Christ's strong nail-scarred hand can grip and hold you.

What has been the time of the church's greatest influence?

Not the days of visible might and splendor; not the days succeeding Constantine when Christianity became imperialistic and the kingdoms of the world and their glory seemed ready to bow beneath the scepter of Christ.

Not the days of the great medieval pontiffs, when the Pope in Rome wielded a sovereignty more absolute than any secular monarch on earth.

Not the days of sunshine, when things have gone well with the church, but rather in the times when it has cried out to God from the depths.

As someone has said, "The blood of the martyrs is the seed of the church." When the church has counted all things but loss, in a Saint Francis, a Martin Luther, a John Wesley, the time of the singing of birds has come, and the whole atmosphere has been full of the Hallelujahs of revival!

"When these things come to pass, look up." Why? Because "your redemption draweth nigh."

CHAPTER 3

Food for Thought

For the world's redemption there is no question between Christ and somebody else. It is Christ or nobody.

He alone can break the love and power of sin. He alone can make a bad man good and the leper clean. He alone can make a poor man rich and a rich man richer, a sick man well and a dead man alive.

Let me sound it out where every lost sheep can hear the call, where every wandering prodigal son can hear his Father's voice: "Seek the Lord while He may be found."

The Bible teaches not only is it impossible to identify life with things, but that things may become a serious hindrance to life.

Life cannot be identified with length of days.

Life is not simply a biological phenomenon.

Millions now living are dead already.

We put wealth and power together and we get, according to the world's standards, greatness. But God's Word teaches us otherwise.

It is not the words we say, the creeds we recite, nor the service we render. When a person subdues his natural arrogance and walks before God in humility and mercy; when he has a heart quick to suffer, to sympathize, and to help; when a person makes a circle of love big enough to include all others and is willing to put others before self—then life begins to reflect the spirit of our Lord Jesus Christ.

We are either dead in sin or alive to Christ. Take any two men, the one a sinner, the other a Christian. Clearly there is bound to be a difference in their outlook and philosophy. But do we have any right to say, as the New Testament says that between these two there is the difference between being dead and being alive? Doesn't it look as if those writers of the New Testament, carried away with the fervor of the newly converted, have allowed their rhetoric to outrun their logic?

Ask anyone who has gone the way of sin, then found Christ. The answer will be "Only then did I begin to live."

Some day we must all stand before our Creator to give an account of the way we have lived.

The Lord of life who created us; the God of mercy who sustains us; the God of wisdom who guides us; the God of perfect holiness who demands of us a perfect heart; the God from whom men flee and for whom they grope as a last refuge; the God whom the wicked desecrate by profanity and blasphemy; the God whom the ungrateful reject despite His blessings; the God whom sinners defy by denying His existence and challenging His authority—that God is Lord.

You and I must inevitably face Him and give an account no matter how self-confident and self-sufficient we may be.

The Sadducees took a more prominent part in the death of Jesus than did the Pharisees. In Acts it is the Sadducees who are hostile to the infant church.

The hostility of the Sadducees was due, not so much to dislike of the doctrine of the resurrection as to selfish and political motives.

Dr. Mendell Taylor said they were "sad, you see" because they didn't believe in the resurrection.

Many of us fail to realize that it's possible at any age to improve the quality of our lives. Let's think of this as a kind of creative arithmetic, with addition, subtraction, multiplication, and division.

1. Add to your life by trying something new.
2. Add to your life by turning limitations into opportunities. For example, when an accident confined Jim to a wheel chair he was overwhelmed by a feeling of uselessness. A woman asked him if she could give his phone number to her daughter's teacher in case of emergency. Word got around. Soon he operated an answering service for other working mothers as well.
3. Subtract from your life things that dim your spiritual vision, for example, jealousy and half-heartedness.
4. Subtract possessions that are a burden, activities you no longer enjoy, and things that cause hang-ups.
5. Multiply your point of contact with others—your connections with life around you.
6. Divide your material and spiritual blessings with others.

Where Jesus was no one ever knew what to expect at any minute. The miraculous, the impossible, were always surprising the disciples as well as the crowds.

His friends felt that if He were beside them, anything and everything was possible. The greatest temptation could be overcome, their worst enemies could be overthrown, and the most critical disease could be healed. His presence brought joy and assurance.

In the days of His flesh no one ever thought of Him as

ineffective or insignificant. Some objected to Him, hated Him, and wanted to get rid of Him. But no one questioned His power.

That same Jesus, with that same power is moving among us now. He who helped His followers in time past is present to help us today.

The Son of Man is going to come in His Father's glory with His angels. At His coming He will be the Judge of all nations.

He divides humanity into two groups—believers and unbelievers—the sheep and the goats. Believers will receive rewards; unbelievers will receive punishment.

Jesus gives a serious warning to those who reject Him and those who are neglectful and unfaithful in their stewardship and service.

You must spend eternity somewhere. Where you spend it is far more important than where you spend this life. Whether you live in a mansion or in poverty, it matters little in comparison to where you will spend eternity.

You will spend eternity in heaven or in hell. The decision is yours, but it must be settled in this life. Your eternal destiny is determined by what you do with Jesus.

A famous painting of Satan and a man playing chess hung in an art gallery. Visitors looking at the picture saw that Satan was winning the game. They shook their heads and said, "That poor fellow doesn't have a chance."

One day a chess expert came to see the painting. He studied it intently for several minutes. Finally, he smiled and said, "There's one move that man can make and beat the Devil."

There's one move we can make to beat Satan. We can flee to Jesus Christ.

> "The hour cometh when the dead shall hear the voice of the Son of God" (John 5:25).

That voice speaks, and strange and mighty things happen. It says, "Let there be light!" And light appears. It commands an evil spirit, "Come out of the man!" And instantly the demon-possessed man is as gentle as a child. It shouts above the roar of the storm, "Peace! Be still!" And immediately there is a great calm. It calls into the tomb of a dead man, "Lazarus, come forth!" And Lazarus walks out into the light.

That voice still speaks today. Sometimes it is a still, small voice, a whisper of hope when all is dark, to comfort, to encourage, and to dispel the shadows from the soul. Sometimes it is a trumpet call, a masterful and strong voice. Sometimes it murmurs, "Come, weary soul, and live." Sometimes it blazes forth in triumph and strength: "Rise up, O man of God. Gird on thine armour and fight."

Whatever its tone, it tells of life made new. And they that hear shall live.

In the Roman Empire a census was taken, usually every seven years, with the double object of assessing taxes and discovering those who were liable for compulsory military service.

Jews were exempt from military service; therefore, in Palestine a census was predominantly for taxation purposes.

The journey from Nazareth to Jerusalem was about 80 miles. People brought their own food. All an innkeeper provided was a place to sleep, fodder for the animals, and a fire for cooking.

"Why did all this happen to me?" We often ask that question. No one knows all the answers. Perhaps the most logical one is "because I am human."

But Jesus not only *has* the answer, He *is* the answer to all of life's questions. He not only *can* help us, He *will* help us. He is our Lord. He knows us by name, and He knows every situation we face. Regardless of our difficulties we can trust Him, for He has everything under control.

While it is understood that the Gospel of Matthew was not the first account to be written; nevertheless, it comes at the beginning of the New Testament because of the importance of the message it portrays and the way it bridges the gap between the Old Testament and the New. It was a leading Gospel in the Early Church.

In his opening chapter, Matthew is careful to show a pattern, then a purpose. A pattern by tracing the royal line of Jesus through David to Abraham, which, in itself, qualifies Jesus to be the Messiah. A purpose, in the manner and nature of His birth.

Matthew's concern is to show that the coming of Jesus was the fulfillment of Old Testament prophecy. Note his frequent references "that it might be fulfilled."

What God had promised, He had fulfilled. The royal line; the Virgin birth; the time, place, and manner of His birth are proof that God had kept His word. Christ had come!

In John 1: 35-39 we read the word of the first disciple. We see John the Baptist pointing beyond himself to Jesus as the Messiah. Once Jesus emerged on the scene, John never had any other thought than to send men to Him.

One day two of John's disciples followed Jesus at a respectable distance. Jesus turned to meet them and asked, "What are you looking for?" He probably caught them off guard.

It might be well for us to ask that question every now and then. Some are searching for security. Some are looking for power, prominence, prestige, or prosperity. Others are looking for peace.

"Rabbi," they asked, "Where are you staying?"

Jesus answered, "Come and see."

They wanted to linger and talk. It was about four o'clock in the afternoon, we're told. Why did John tell us what time it was? The time was important because no one can forget the day and the hour when Christ becomes a reality, when all things become new.

Suppose the apostles were to come back to earth today and watch us at our weekly worship. Would they recognize the religion in whose dawn they had found it such bliss to be alive? Perhaps they might ask, "What has happened?"

"Is this the faith that once stirred the world like a thousand trumpets?

"How can these descendants of ours hear the message of God's grace and mercy and be bored?

"Can they sit through a moving message on God's love or the resurrection of Christ and not be thrilled and dazzled by the telling of it?

"Can they really say, 'Christ is risen!' and not want to shout for the glory of it?

"Does the zeal for God's house no longer devour them?"

The stars we look at watched the founding and the passing of Babylon, Ninevah, Persia, Greece, and Rome.

They saw Joseph take on the royal purple and Pharoah put on sackcloth. They took note of Socrates in the Academia and of Abraham in his long pilgrimage. They looked down upon Daniel in the den of lions. They saw Paul and Silas in their jail cell at midnight

They saw the Pyramids rising from the Egyptian desert. They saw kings and pharaohs laid in their sarcophagi. New dynasties arose and others superseded them. No less than nineteen civilizations have gone to their graves at the point where they left God out of their plans.

Still the silent Pyramids stand, but the dynasties which reared them are gone and forgotten. Still men walk through the Forum and stand amid the ruins of the old Colosseum, but barbarians from the north overwhelmed the mistress of the world and dragged her generals at their chariot wheels.

Even the sun, moon, and stars shall themselves pass away. Some day they will strew the ashes of their undoing along the path where once they blazed in glory.

I take my inspiration from Him who passed across a narrow corner of an obscure and subject land and left His footprints there so deep and unmistakable that the ages have not obliterated them.

The smoke and fog of error and sin may lie for a while across the way before us; but one breath from the hills of truth will sweep it away, and God's great stars will shine on in holy calm.

A.W. Tozer wrote: "Religion today is not transforming the people; rather it is being transformed by the people. It is not raising the moral level of society; it is descending to society's own level and congratulating itself that it has scored a victory because society is smilingly accepting its surrender."

God. The Almighty One! He whose name is love, whose delight is mercy, and whose whole being is holiness and light, far excels all we can ever tell of Him.

With a God who knows the way through and asks only that we follow, there isn't much room for bewilderment!

Since it is God and you together, you can face your problem or trial and see it through with honor and victory.

You are each, in the sight of God, original, unique, and irreplaceable. As yet you are not the real person God wants you to be, but only a bundle of possibilities out of which that all can be fashioned.

Jesus' words seem yet to echo in the air. The passing of centuries have not hushed His voice. None of His words have lost any of their power.

How could they fail, when no man ever spoke as He spoke?

The greatest Teacher of all the ages speaks. He speaks of the kingdom of God. He shows us that it is not a structure to be built; it is not a thesis to be defended; it is instead a life to be developed.

Some men spend the greater part of their lives putting limitations on the power of God. But with Him all things are possible; the word *impossible* has no place in the Christian's vocabulary.

There was always something daring about Jesus. He loved to fling down a challenge before impossible situations.

In the porches of Bethesda, He looked for no cheap and easy way to make a reputation by healing some neurotic woman with nothing really wrong with her, except that she had too little to do.

But He found His way, in all that group of sufferers, to the very worst and most nearly hopeless case in the place.

In looking forward to His death, Jesus had spoken of it as the way to something much greater. The women and the apostles had been told again and again that He would rise; yet the women came bringing spices to anoint His dead body and the apostles hid behind closed doors.

More space is devoted in the Gospels to an account of Christ's resurrection than to any other aspect of His life except the trial and crucifixion.

The conflict of the centuries has raged around Jesus Christ. God was unknown until Jesus came, walked in our midst, and communed with us. He ate with sinners, touched elbows with profane and wicked men, healed the sick, made the lame to leap with joy, and brought unlimited happiness.

Jesus taught new and revolutionary doctrines. He taught that it is possible to *have* much and *be* little. He taught that it is possible to become so busy acquiring material possessions, or making a living, that we miss life.

He taught that wealth is too often a vulgar vanity that molds those who possess it into its own likeness.

He said it would be better to beg for bread in this life than to beg for water in hell.

He taught us that He is the world's Savior, and there is no other.

If this were your last year and you knew it, what would you do? As for me, eternal salvation would be my top priority. I would want to cling loosely to things that perish. I would want to have a forgiving spirit toward everybody. I'd want to become more wrapped up in my family and my church.

Make your own list. It could lead to the best year of your life.

We have been thinking we could skip character and live on the morals of our forefathers; the truth is we can't.

We have a generation with less and less respect for parents and with less and less respect for God.

No one has ever found sin to pay. No new sins have been discovered, and no old ones have gone out of style.

In Psalms 19:1, David describes the heavens as a grand cathedral and every star a preacher speaking forth the glory of the Divine Architect who made it and set it where it shines.

The hands of God's timepiece never vary the smallest fraction of a second. And every planet in its orbit, every sun and star, every moon and meteor obeys His will as it speeds in orderly fashion across the unlimited stretches of the universe. We stand amazed in the presence of such a marvel as this!

What is man? Really he is a mere speck in this universe of monstrous measurements. And yet, for some reason, God is mindful of him and manifests Himself in mercy to him. Long before God swung the suns and moons and stars into place, He made for man the universe and all that is in it.

Our Father Creator made us in His own image. He gave us a mind that could think, a heart that could love, and a will that could choose.

It's great to have a God like the One the heavens reveal!

We Christians may not see eye to eye, but we can walk arm in arm.

A day without noticing something beautiful is like walking through a tunnel.

We change our minds about religion when we get into trouble and have no God.

No smart man ever takes flattery or criticism at full face value.

How difficult it is for the finite to grasp the Infinite; for the earthly to comprehend the heavenly; for the sinful to approach the holy! Where do we begin? How do we proceed? Where do we leave off?

As we read the records of His life that we have available today, there is no doubt that Christ is God manifest in the flesh.

The difference between courtship and marriage is the difference between pictures in a seed catalog and what comes up.

Marriage is like vitamins. We supplement each other's minimum daily requirements.

There is no such thing as a non-working mother.

"I have found that the best way to give advice to your children is to find out what they want, and then advise them to do it."
—Harry Truman

"No matter how much cats fight, there always seem to be plenty of kittens."
—Abraham Lincoln

A happy home is one in which each spouse grants that the other may be right, though neither believes it.

If in the last few years you haven't discarded a major opinion or acquired a new one, check your pulse. You may be dead.

Teach a child to be polite and courteous in the home, and when he grows up, he'll never be able to edge his car onto a freeway.

In the old days if a kid was in the principal's office, it meant the kid was in trouble. Now it means the principal is in trouble.

Getting married is easy. Staying married is more difficult. Staying happily married for a lifetime ranks among the fine arts.

There are only two things we can do with the Christian faith: give it away, or give it up.

What this world needs is a computer that can figure out all the things in life that don't add up.

We owe it to the world to be as good as it thinks we are.

Jesus came to tell us that God loves us; bad as we are, we are still dear to God.

Daniel Webster once said that the strongest argument he knew for religion was an old aunt of his.

It is not so much God sending judgment on men as a man who brings judgment on himself when he has no place for God in his scheme of things.

People have tried to take the shame out of sin, the fire out of hell, the wrath out of divine judgment, and the reality out of eternal retribution.

In the past, we talked less about living our lives and more about saving our souls. But today the emphasis has shifted from the religious and the moral to the political and economic.

The attraction toward heaven has decreased, and the gravitation toward earth has increased. The single search for God has given way to the double quest for Power and Wealth.

It is evident that, since we can't fit Jesus into our plans, we must do one of two things: fit ourselves into His world or let Him go.

The Bible has a proper understanding of the wonder of the heavens and the glory of the world. But it is not so much impressed with nature's majesty as with the God who heals the broken-hearted and lifts up the fallen.

We like to think of our churches as established institutions like banks or post offices, but they are not. They are mission stations on the frontier of faith.

God created human beings to have fellowship with Him and to enjoy His blessings. He has put some knowledge of Himself and how to live in every man.

Those who have not found the daily presence of God and the sort of life that Christ makes possible are spending their time on earth without ever knowing why they were born. They are missing the greatest good that life can give.

It is remarkable how we come back to the New Testament for our standard and our inspiration.

How poor and confused is man! He thinks that sound means power; noise means progress; big things mean mighty things.

Knowledge of Christianity does not make one a Christian, but one cannot be a Christian without it.

How can we expect to know the reality of religion when we do so little to make it a vital force in our lives?

The greatest teaching of the ages was not done by scholars and scientists, but it has been the teaching of Jesus, the Nazarene, enforced and enlarged by the Fisherman of Galilee and The Tentmaker of Tarsus.

Psychologists say that happiness stems from usefulness. Happy people are busy people. Happy are those who enjoy being useful in places where they are needed.

George W. Childs said, "Don't keep your alabaster boxes of love and tenderness sealed up until your friends are dead. Fill their lives with sweetness now. Speak approving, cheering words while their ears can hear them and while their hearts can be thrilled and made happier by them."

Although the world may seem like a huge globe to us, if God should send an angel out to find our planet Earth, it would be like sending a child out to find one particular grain of sand on the beach. It is all so vast and we are so small.

There is no such thing as absolute freedom. There is only the choice of whom you will serve—Jesus Christ or Satan.

You can serve Satan in the prison house of sin, or you can serve Christ in the green pastures and beside the still waters. Serving Christ means freedom to do what He wants you to do and to be what He wants you to be.

God has provided salvation for every soul through Christ, and He offers that salvation to all people on terms they can meet. If you fail to comply with these conditions, you are responsible for your own damnation.

From the way we hear people talk and from the way they act, we are led to imagine that the only prosperity that is worthwhile is material prosperity. But is it? The Bible says, "Man shall not live by bread alone." Bread sustains life, but what is life? Life is really the new relationship that we have with God.

Remember, after all, it's God's road we're on, and often as not that road is a long uphill road that takes us past Golgotha and sometimes by the way of the wilderness or a bed of pain.

The Christian faith centers in a definite Person by the name of Jesus of Nazareth. Christianity is definitely a supernatural religion. It rests upon the affirmation that a series of events happened in which God revealed Himself for the salvation of the race. All we really know about Christ while He was here on earth, we know from the four gospels: Matthew, Mark, Luke, and John.

For many people, religion has lost that characteristic of positive certainty. They may give assent to its existence, but they do not feel any of its vital force. When people do not feel the vital force of religion, it is not real for them.

Insofar as we lose the sense of the reality of our Christian faith, to that extent we are on the way to abandoning it. But suppose something like the Damascus Road experience of St. Paul occurs in your life. Then all of religion and all of life are vastly different.

God sits aloft and holds the reins of the universe. He is in the mysterious things of life. I confess I am not able to understand all His dealings with men. If I could understand all that God is and what men are, I might solve all mysteries.

I do not know why one of the greatest musicians was deaf and couldn't hear his own compositions played.

I do not know why one of the greatest poets was blind.

I do not know why Jacob had to weep over the stained garment of his son.

I cannot tell why Joseph had to go to prison as the only way to mount the throne.

I don't understand why when St. Paul prayed for the removal of a thorn in the flesh, it wasn't removed.

I don't understand why Jesus had to suffer and die for our salvation.

But I must hold all questions until the morning after the resurrection, when all the evidence is in and we shall know as we are known.

The trouble is not that we deny the existence of God, but that God just does not count.

CHAPTER 4

Anecdotes

In his book *How to Stop Worrying and Start Living,* Dale Carnegie gives the two following illustrations:

A woman named Thelma Thompson from New York had a life-changing experience during the war.

Her husband was stationed at an army training camp in the Mojave Desert in California.

She said, "I went to live there so I could be near him. I hated the place! I loathed it! I had never been so miserable before. My husband was on maneuvers, and I was left in the tiny shack alone, the heat was unbearable, 125 in the shade of a cactus.

"There was not a soul to talk to but Mexicans and Indians, and they couldn't speak English. The wind blew and there was lots of sand in it.

"I was so utterly wretched, and so sorry for myself that I wrote to my parents and told them I couldn't stand it, and I was coming home. I'd rather be in jail than to stay there.

"My father wrote back with just two lines.

'Two men looked out from prison bars,
One saw mud, the other saw stars.'

"I read those two lines over, and I was ashamed of myself. I made up my mind I would find the stars. I would find out what was good about my present situation.

"I made friends with the natives and their reaction astonished me. When I showed an interest in their weaving and pottery, they gave me presents of their best pieces which they wouldn't sell to tourists.

"I studied the fascinating forms of the cactus and the yuccas and Joshua trees. I learned about prairie dogs and watched for the desert sunsets.

Life was so exciting that I wrote a book about the desert, a novel, published under the title of *Bright Ramparts*.

"What brought about this astonishing change in me? The Mojave Desert hadn't changed. The Indians hadn't changed, but I had, and this wretched experience became the most exciting adventure of my whole life. I had looked out of my self-created prison and saw the stars."

The second story:

"I once visited a happy farmer down in Florida who turned a lemon into lemonade. When he first got the farm he was discouraged. The land was poor. He couldn't grow fruit or even raise pigs. He just had a lot of scrub oaks and rattlesnakes. He decided to make the most out of those rattlesnakes.

"To the amazement of everyone, he started canning rattlesnake meat.

"Soon tourists were pouring in from everywhere to see his rattlesnake farm, 20,000 a year.

"He shipped poison from the fangs of those snakes to laboratories to make anti-venom toxin.

"I saw rattlesnake skins being sold at fancy prices to make women's shoes and handbags. Canned rattlesnake meat was shipped to customers all over the world.

"I bought a picture post card of the place and mailed it at the local post office there which had been re-named 'Rattlesnake, Florida,' in honor of this man who had overcome such obstacles."

Rita Snowden tells the following story, which shows what love can do.

During the last world war in Europe there had been a battle with a few casualties in France. Some soldiers, with their sergeant, brought the body of a dead comrade to a French cemetery to bury their friend there.

The priest told them gently that it was a Roman Catholic cemetery, and he should ask if the dead man was a baptized Catholic. They said they didn't know whether he was or not. The priest said he was very sorry, but in that case he could not permit burial in his churchyard.

So the soldiers buried their friend just outside the fence of the churchyard.

The next day they came back to see that the grave was all right. To their astonishment they couldn't find it. They knew it was only six feet from the graveyard fence, but they could find no trace of freshly dug soil by the fence.

As they turned to leave in bewilderment, the priest came up to them. He told them his heart had been troubled because he had refused to have the soldier buried in the churchyard. So he got up very early the next morning and moved the fence to include the body of the soldier who had died for France.

Rules and regulations had put up the fence. But love had removed it.

Edgerton Young was the first missionary to the Indians in Saskatchewan. He went out over the hills and ridges to visit them and to tell them about the love of our Heavenly Father. To those Indians this was a new revelation of God.

After the missionary's message one day, an old chief said to him, "When you spoke of the Great Spirit just now, did I hear you say, 'Our Father?'"

"Yes," said the missionary.

"That is very new and sweet to me," said the chief. "We've never thought of the Great Spirit as Father. We heard Him in the thunder; we saw Him in the lightning, in the storms and in the blizzard, and we were afraid, so when you tell us the Great Spirit is our father that is very beautiful to us."

The old chief paused; then he went on as a new thought seemed to come to him. "Missionary," he said, "Did you say the Great Spirit is *your* father?"

"Yes," said the missionary.

"And did you say He was the *Indian's* father?"

"I did," Edgerton said.

"If He is your Father and my Father, too," said the old chief, "that makes us *brothers.*"

The story is told of the French politician, Renaud, who had been elected to the French Senate.

After his election, he left his home in the Pyrenees for Paris, where he took a room in a leading hotel and paid a month's rent in advance. The rent was one hundred and fifty francs.

The hotel clerk asked if he would like a receipt.

"It isn't necessary," said Renaud. "God has witnessed this transaction."

"Do you believe in God?" the clerk asked.

"Most assuredly," said the senator. "Don't you?"

"No, not I, monsieur," the clerk answered.

"Well, in that case," the senator said, "will you please give me a receipt?"

The story is told of a harp that hung in the palace of a prince. No one ever played it because it was so far out of tune that it made such harsh, discordant sounds, and no one could be found who could tune it.

Years passed. The beautiful instrument was covered with a cloth and almost hidden from view.

But one day a guest came to the castle. He noticed the harp and asked why it was covered. When someone explained the reason, the guest said, "Would you mind if I tried to tune it, please!" The curtain was removed.

The old man examined the harp carefully and handled it

fondly as if it were a child. For more than an hour he worked away. Then he asked the prince to assemble the entire household, for he felt sure that the harp which was so badly out of tune and made such harsh music was its self once more.

The man played beautiful music. Everyone was completely enthralled. No one ever dreamed of hearing music like that coming from that old harp.

When the prince could compose himself, he said, "Sir, how does it happen that when all other musicians failed in tuning the harp, you have done so wonderfully?"

The old man replied, "It's all very simple. I made the harp."

There is One who can touch the discordant strings of our hearts and bring them all into harmony with the will of heaven. Who could it be but the One who made us?

A preacher told a story about a nationally famous radio commentator who was a guest at the Chamber of Commerce in his city. After the luncheon the commentator told the preacher about the following incident.

He said that years ago when he was just a young fellow he was on a ranch in the west. He remembered one little, big-eared, bowlegged cowboy on that ranch, who was about the most broken-hearted, miserable man he had ever seen.

The cowboy had raised a colt, which had grown to be a big, fine stallion. He and the horse loved each other very much. Everybody teased the cowboy about his horse. It would follow him around like a dog.

The horse had stepped into a gopher hole and sprained his ankle and had been put out in the big pasture. Some wild horses had broken into the pasture and broken out again, and this favorite horse had gone with them. So the cowboy was heart-broken.

The next evening one of the ranch hands raced into the yard at the big house. He yelled to the dejected little cowboy that his horse had been found.

"He's with a herd of wild horses not far from here, down in the canyon," the man said.

It was late, so the little cowboy got ready to go before daylight the next morning.

The radio commentator said, "I persuaded him to let me go along.

"We got on top of the rim-rock so we could look down the canyon and decide how best to stalk his horse. We could see horses grazing quietly.

"I watched as the little cowboy went down on foot into the canyon. He eased up close enough for his voice to reach his horse. Then he called.

"I saw the horse lift his head, and all of the others were suddenly on the alert, their heads up. I knew he was talking to his horse for all he was worth. Then the herd bolted and ran, all but one. He stood still, but he didn't know what to do. He looked at the other horses and took a step or two. Then he looked back at the cowboy, pranced around a little; then he looked again.

"I could feel that it must have been terrible for the horse to decide. There was the master whom he dearly loved, and there was the wild herd with which he had run. Which way should he go?

"I thought for a moment the cowboy had lost. The horse took half a dozen steps as if to catch up with the herd. Then he stopped and looked back, and with his head up and his neck arched, he came trotting to his master.

"The cowboy put a rope around his neck, patted and caressed him, and cried a little too I discovered later. The cowboy reached into his pocket and brought out a lump or two of sugar for his horse."

Then the preacher said that the well known news commentator looked at him and said, "Preacher, I just laid my head down on my hands up there at the edge of the canyon, and I prayed, 'O Lord, if ever I am tempted to run with the wild crowd in life, Dear Lord, let me listen to my Master's voice and let me come back to Him.' That was my prayer then, and that's been my prayer ever since!"

As business associates, long-time acquaintances, and curious observers filed past the ornate casket, nobody pulled out a handkerchief to wipe a tear. Only Mr. Johnson's brother, sister-in-law, and a nephew sat in the section reserved for relatives. No tears there either.

His wife's two young lady pastors conducted the service. My husband and I, evangelists for a youth revival, sang.

A few blocks away, in separate hospital rooms only a few doors apart, the two real mourners no doubt wept silently. One, his wife, had no hope that he had made peace with God. The other, his mistress, knew that she had played the fool. Upon hearing of his heart attack, she had taken poison. The sleek new Buick he had bought for her had lost its attraction. Within forty-eight hours she would follow her lover into eternity.

Thus ended in irony and infamy a life once used of God. Mr. Johnson had been a devout Christian. He organized a church and served as its pastor in that little Texas city.

But something went terribly wrong. Love of money? Desire for prestige? A lustful eye? Perhaps all of these contributed to his downfall.

At first his flagrant love affair with a younger woman met with criticism and contempt. Gradually, however, most of the townspeople accepted this backslidden pastor and his mistress. "After all," some men reasoned, "his wife is older than he and she isn't well."

Despite her husband's infidelity, Mrs. Johnson remained faithful to God and to her marriage vows. She continued to pray for her husband's salvation and to support her church and pastors.

In the meantime, he bought a new Buick for his mistress and a casket for his wife. Little did he suspect he would be buried in it.

Although readily admitting his backslidden condition, Mr. Johnson treated his wife's pastors with respect. Often when "the girls," as he called them, visited in the home, he would give them money for the church.

During one of their visits, Mr. Johnson told them about a conversation he had with a pastor of another denomination in town.

"I said to Pastor Howard, 'You *know* I used to be a Christian, but if I died I'd go to hell. Some of your members are doing the same things I'm doing; but, if they died you'd preach them right into heaven.'"

During the fall revival before Mr. Johnson's death, the evangelist's wife became deeply concerned about his soul. She asked the pastors to go with her to talk to him.

As they pled with him, he said, "Girls, why are you pressing me so?"

"Because the revival is almost over," one lady said.

"There'll be another one!" he retorted.

He was right; there was another revival. But he died the night before it started.

My husband and I had barely arrived that Saturday afternoon when the pastors told us about Mr. Johnson. The previous Sunday morning he had gone to the hospital to visit his wife. While waiting in the lounge, he suffered a massive heart attack and was placed in the room across the hall from his wife. He had shown no evidence of consciousness—unless possibly he had tried to squeeze the hand of a man who went to see him. "The girls" were extremely concerned about his spiritual welfare. They wanted us to go with them to the hospital just in case a man's voice might penetrate his consciousness and we could pray with him.

As we entered the hospital in that small city, the sound of this poor man's struggle for breath reverberated throughout the hospital. We stepped into his room. My husband reached for his hand and spoke. No response, of course. A few minutes later, the telephone rang at the parsonage. Mr. Johnson was gone.

After the funeral, the pastors visited Mrs. Johnson at the hospital. In the lobby they met Pastor Howard coming back from her room.

"Well, Ladies," he said, "I believe the old man made it."

"We have only his testimony for it," one of the pastors said.

The words of Solomon still echo through more than half a century: "And I saw the wicked buried, who had come and gone from the place of the holy, and they were forgotten in the city where they had so done" (Eccl. 8:10).

[Names have been changed to protect identities].

Dr. Norman Vincent Peale told of an incident that happened in the early days of his ministry at Marble Collegiate Church.

He said, "I received a telephone call asking me to come to a home on Riverside Drive. As I stopped my car in the driveway and looked at the palatial mansion, I wondered what could trouble anyone who had a lovely home such as this.

"A servant opened the door and ushered me into the spacious living room. Evidence of wealth was everywhere. Several lovely works of art adorned the walls. As I waited for the lady who called me, I couldn't resist walking over to stand in front of one of the paintings. I was lost in its beauty when she entered and spoke. I apologized, and said, 'Anyone who has the privilege of living in a room like this must be grateful and happy.'

"Without a word she walked over to a mahogany table in the center of the room and opened a drawer. She took out a pearl-handled revolver and laid it on the table then turned very slowly to face me.

"She said, 'Dr. Peale, I would have used this on myself but for the embarrassment it would have caused my family and friends. I am utterly miserable inside. Everything you think is so attractive in this house is overshadowed by the misery that is in my heart.'"

Dr. Peale went on to say that material things alone were never intended to make life full and happy.

The greatest philosopher whom America has produced in a hundred years, Borden P. Browne, was professor of philosophy at Boston University. For a time he was a member of a philosophic club which met in Cambridge on the campus of Harvard.

Browne was a believer in the Virgin Birth of Christ, and his fellow philosophers often taunted him about his beliefs. One day one of them said, "Browne, suppose an unmarried young woman here in Cambridge should be discovered pregnant, and suppose she might be asked who is the father of her child; and suppose she would say that the child has no father except God. What would you say? Would you believe her?"

Professor Browne thought for a moment, and then he answered something like this: "I'd probably do what you would; I would probably say that she was lying. BUT if I could live for many years after the birth of that child, and if I could observe Him grow up to be a strong, courageous, good man; if I could see Him become absolutely the world's greatest teacher; if I could see Him do wonderful things beyond the power of anyone else to do or to understand; if I could hear His words of hope and forgiveness and peace; if I could observe Him loving His enemies, blessing the ones who cursed Him and took His life.

"If I could see Him patiently bearing all manner of suffering, then be put to death on a Roman cross, an innocent man, dying as Jesus did; and then know that three days later all His friends were convinced that He was alive beyond death, . . . I think then that I would listen again to what that young mother had said, and allow myself to think that perhaps, after all, she had been telling the truth."

Shortly after World War I a newspaper in Chicago came out with a story that the young daughter of a local millionaire was paralyzed. She couldn't walk and had no hope of walking again. The family sent her to the greatest specialists, surgeons, and sanitariums in the country but it was to no avail.

Just about that time there arose into prominence a great Austrian physician, Dr. Lorenz. The girl's father paid him twenty thousand dollars as a fee and brought him to America. He operated on the girl, and she was able to walk again. She had a slight limp, but it was hardly noticeable.

In those days in Chicago, back of the stockyards, there was a section called the Shanty Irish section. It was dirt poor, poorer than the poor.

In the poorest of that section, there lived a widow and her fourteen-year-old son, Michael. He, too, had paralysis—got it from an accident. He was confined to bed. They were so poor that they couldn't buy a wheel chair. The mother would carry him to the table or outside for a breath of fresh air.

One day the mother came home from work and found Michael sitting in bed, crying, a newspaper spread out on his knees.

"What's the matter, Michael?" his mother asked. She looked at the paper—the ordinary strikes, automobile accidents, divorces, hold-ups.

Michael pointed to an article describing the marvelous cure of the rich man's daughter.

"Son, that is something to praise the saints over," the mother said.

"Mama, wouldn't it be wonderful if that doctor would operate on me, and I could walk?"

The heart of that poor mother rose in her throat. "They paid him twenty thousand dollars and we don't have hardly twenty cents," she said.

Michael looked up and said, "Mama, can't a guy even wish?"

His mother could stand no more. Running out the door, she leaned against the house and wept. God gave her an idea.

She went down town to Michigan Boulevard, walked into the Blackstone Hotel, and asked for the doctor's suite. She threw herself on her knees before that doctor.

He could hardly speak English, but between him and his secretary they learned what she wanted. He quieted her down and asked her some questions.

He said, "Madam, do you have any money?"

She threw herself down again and did everything but kiss his shoes and kept pleading and begging.

"Not for me," said Dr. Lorenz: "I don't want any money. It is to go to the hospital for the X-ray and laboratory, for bandages and nurses."

The mother kept crying.

Dr. Lorenz turned to his secretary and said something. The secretary got his hat and coat. He took the woman home. He examined Michael, made him scream with pain once or twice, then called an ambulance and took him to the West Side Free Hospital.

Dr. Lorenz stayed over here for eleven weeks, working on that boy. And he walked!

Michael said, "Doctor, as long as there is a tongue to wag in my head, there ain't nobody ever going to hear the last of what you have done for me."

How can a Christian for whom the Lord has provided salvation keep from telling others about Him?

Santa Teresa—known as Mother Teresa—was one of the most influential women who ever lived. For many years she was just an ordinary, unknown nun, going through her religious duties day by day, correctly enough, but, as she said later, mechanically and coldly and formally with hardly a touch of soul in it all.

Then one day, very much the same as hundreds of other days, as she was entering the chapel, as she had done so many times before, her eyes chanced to fall on the Crucifix. But this time, somehow, she really saw it. She took in the meaning and wonder of it, that it is only by the cross and by the wondrous love of God that we can be saved.

Flinging herself on her knees, she dedicated herself then and there—holding back absolutely nothing—to the service of her marvelous Lord. She began a new and thrilling volume in her life, which from that hour kept taking her deeper and still deeper into communion with God and fellowship with Jesus Christ and giving herself to service for her fellow men.

She has since been given the Nobel Prize for her work in India among the very poor and unfortunate.

She was responsible for 7500 children in 60 schools; 1600 abandoned orphans in 20 homes; 3400 destitute or dying in 23 homes; 47,000 victims of leprosy in 54 clinics and 213 dispensaries in 35 cities or towns in India and elsewhere.

Her first project—a home for the destitute and dying—started when she saw an old woman, bitten by rats, covered with ants, dying in the street.

The Waldensian preachers sometimes traveled about as merchants and dealt in jewels and precious stones as a way of obtaining access to families of the nobility.

When they had disposed of their rings and trinkets and were asked if they had nothing more to sell, they answered, "Yes, we have jewels still more precious than any you have seen. We will be glad to show you these also if you will promise not to betray us to the clergy. We have here a precious stone so brilliant that by its light a man may see God." Then, unwrapping their bundle, they brought out a Bible.

The Double Cure

> "For he hath made him to be sin for us, who knew no sin; that we might be made the righteousness of God in him" (II Cor. 5: 21).

This story was written by J.D. Peacock many years ago. It's a perfect illustration of our predicament today.

In 1893 in Sing Sing prison there was a man named Bill Caesar. Bill had been found guilty of murder in the first degree, and sentenced to be electrocuted. When a new trial was denied him he had taken his case to the Supreme Court of the State of New York, where, after months of delay, the decision of the lower court had been sustained. Finally, by mortgaging his home and everything else and raising all the money he could from friends, old Bill had been able to get his briefs printed and his case was carried to the United States Supreme Court at Washington. All this time he was in jail going through the most awful piece of torture, waiting for the return of the case in the United States Supreme Court. After a long delay word came that here also the decision of the lower court had been sustained. There was no hope for him and old Bill absolutely collapsed.

Just One Bright Ray

He discovered one tiny ray of hope, however. He reasoned, "If I can only get the governor now to give me a reprieve and sentence me to life imprisonment in Sing Sing prison, maybe the state of New York will some day have another governor, and he will give me a pardon." Now that was a little like a drowning man grabbing at a straw which is a good ways off, and yet it was the only hope he had.

After his collapse Bill just simply gave up and went into a decline and finally the doctors declared that this fellow had what they called in 1893, "quick," or "galloping, consumption." We do not have that now; we have "tuberculosis" instead, which is altogether a different thing, and yet which works just the same. But the point is that when Bill got this quick consumption, of course his friends rushed over as fast as they could and they said, "Look here, doctor, you must do everything you can for old Bill and get right at it; give him the best room and all the nurses you have."

The doctor said: "Wait a minute. Why do you suppose I want to kill myself trying to get old Bill Caesar cured? If I cure him he will have to die in the electric chair."

Next they wrote to the governor, saying: "You will have to do something for old Bill, for he has quick consumption. You must pardon him; that is the only thing you can do, and you will have to do it quick. He is all broken down; the man is very sick with this incurable disease."

And the governor said: "Wait a minute. Don't get excited. Why do you suppose I am going to pardon this man Caesar? He will die of his disease. A pardon isn't going to do him any good."

A Double Sentence of Death

Old Bill was under a double sentence of death. If he were cured, he must die for his murder; if he got a pardon, he must die of his disease. A pardon wouldn't help him; a cure wouldn't help him. What he needed was both.

That is the picture of every man, woman and child born into the world since Adam fell. It has always been just one story, that sin is not only a disease, but sin is a crime. A lot of people will tell you to be gentle with certain kinds of sin, like drunkenness, because drunkenness is not a sin, but a disease. All right, but just remember this one thing; when a man is a drunkard, he is a sinner. That is a foregone conclusion.

You know very well that sin is a disease. David once said, "Behold, I was shapen in iniquity; and in sin did my mother conceive me." Isaiah declared, "From the sole of the foot even unto the head there is no soundness in it; but wounds, and bruises, and putrefying sores—a horrible picture. Paul said, "In me (that is, in my flesh,) dwelleth no good thing."

I am old-fashioned enough to believe the Bible from cover to cover. The Bible contains the Word of God. No, the Bible *is* the Word of God: I like it better that way—then I can get my foot on it anywhere and it won't slip. So I am going to keep on believing what God said about original sin. He said, "The soul that sinneth, it shall die." And when He made Adam in His own image He made him without death in him.

Keep the Faith

A ministerial student friend I'll call Sam Johnson was working on a Ph.D. at a Midwestern state university. One day his philosophy professor announced that each student would have an opportunity to present and to defend his/her philosophy in class.

Sam listened intently and silently as all the other students explained and defended their atheistic philosophies. The professor seemed to agree with them. So, when his turn came, Sam expected the worst. Yet he stood before that class of atheists to explain and defend his Christian faith.

After class the professor said, "I want to see you in my office at 2 p.m. tomorrow."

What now? Regardless of the effect his presentation before the class might have on his future, Sam knew he had done what he could to give them the truth.

Still wondering why he was called into the office, Sam kept his appointment.

In amazement, Sam listened as the professor asked if he knew anything about two well known church colleges. Sam said he did.

"In my youth I attended both of those colleges to prepare for the ministry. Then I entered the university and they wrecked my faith."

"Johnson, whatever I say in class, you keep your faith. I am undergoing psychiatric treatment regularly as a result, doctors tell me, of the shock I received when I gave up my faith."

CHAPTER 5

Outlines

Why Conservative Churches Are Growing By Dean Kelley

1. They give people something definite to believe in;
2. They call for a clear commitment;
3. They build a strong sense of fellowship;
4. They challenge their people with missionary zeal.

Seven Promises in Romans 8

1. The "no condemnation" promise (v.1)
2. The resurrection promise (v.11)
3. The "sonship" promise (v.14)
4. The "no comparison" promise (v.18)
5. The "all things" promise (v.28)
6. The "free provision" promise (v.32)
7. The "no separation" promise (vs.35)

Characteristics of the Early Church (Acts 2:42-45)

1. Learning
2. Fellowship
3. Praying
4. Sharing
5. Praising

Spiritual Gifts (Rom. 12: 6-8)

1. Prophesying
2. Serving
3. Teaching
4. Encouraging
5. Contributing to the needs of others
6. Leadership
7. Showing mercy

Paul's Rules for Living (Gal.5-6)

1. Stand firm (5:1)
2. Serve one another in love (5:13)
3. Live by the Spirit (5:16)
4. Keep in step with the Spirit (5:25)
5. Carry each other's burdens (6:2)
6. Don't be weary in well doing (6:9)
7. Do good to all, especially the church family (6:10)

Peter's Advice (I Pet. 1:1-18)

1. Be self-controlled (1:13)
2. Be holy (1:15)
3. Love the brotherhood (1:17)
4. Fear God (1:17)
5. Honor the king (1:17)
6. Submit yourselves (1:18)

Peter's Arithmetic (II Peter 1:5-7)

Add to your faith:

1. Goodness
2. Knowledge
3. Self-control

4. Perseverance
5. Godliness
6. Brotherly kindness
7. Love

Jude's Greetings

Jude addresses his letter to the following Christians:

1. Those who have been called,
2. Those who are loved by God the Father
3. Those who are kept by Jesus Christ.

God Spoke

God spoke to His people by deeds as well as words.

I. He made Himself known to Israel in their history, and so directed their development as to bring to those Israelites His salvation and then His judgment.
II. God rescued the people from their slavery in Egypt. Then He brought them safely across the desert and settled them in the Promised Land.
III. He preserved their national identity through the period of the Judges. He gave them kings to rule over them, in spite of the fact that their demand for a human king was in part a repudiation of His own kingship.
IV. God's judgment came upon them for their constant disobedience when they were deported into Babylonian exile.
V. He restored them to their own land and enabled them to rebuild their nationhood and their temple.
VI. Above all, for their salvation—and for ours—He sent His Son Jesus to be born, to live and to work, to suffer and to die, to rise again and to pour out His Holy Spirit.

Through these methods, first in the Old Testament, then in the New, especially in Jesus Christ, God was actively and purposely revealing Himself.

When God spoke He didn't shout audibly out of the blue sky. He spoke through the prophets in the Old Testament and through the apostles in the New Testament.

The Prodigal and the Son
Luke 15:11-31

Some call this the greatest story in all literature.

It was not unusual for a father to distribute his estate if he wished to retire. But this son asked for his share. He couldn't wait until his father's death to begin squandering his money in the far country.

Put yourself in the place of that prodigal.

1. It took him a while to get there. We have no idea how long it took him to waste his money in riotous living. But once he was broke and friendless, no doubt he was ashamed of himself. He probably shrank from looking people in the face. No doubt he blamed others, possibly heredity or circumstances. Eventually he reached the lowest rung on the ladder to the point that he not only fed pigs, but he craved the slop they were eating. When faced with starvation, he finally came to his senses.
2. He realized that he was not only a prodigal, but he was a son as well. Had he thought of himself only as a prodigal, he would have stayed there in shame and remorse until he starved.

    Deep within himself, he reasoned: "I'm really a son! Despite all this moral failure, that is what I really am. I don't belong here. I will arise and go to my father!"

    The father didn't go after him. He didn't show contempt—slam the door. He didn't even lecture the boy or put him on probation.
3. At home, forgiven, probably for the rest of his days he had

an understanding of and sympathy for boys who were about to go wrong, and he knew just how to help them.
4. Moral failure can be used for positive good. St. Paul started as a persecutor of the church.
5. The reinstated son could tell others that (1) sin is dreadful, not enticing and exciting as it is pictured, (2) it is punished pitilessly, (3) it is shameful, and (4) the only way out is to be forgiven.

Comments about God

To many professing Christians, God is what He was to the Athenians of Paul's day, "the unknown God." The more we know of God, however, the better and more effective our service for Him will be.

Of course no man can know God perfectly. Yet a certain amount of knowledge of God is necessary in order to be saved (Rom.10:17).

The Scriptures do not attempt to prove God's existence. But they reveal Him in various ways.

1. God is a Spirit (John 4:24). As such He is omnipresent. The Psalmist David asked, "Whither shall I go from they spirit? Or whither shall I flee from thy presence?" (Psa.139:7).
2. God is a Person. Personality here does not necessarily include substance as we understand it. It does, however, stand for intelligence, self-determination, reason, will, individuality.
3. God is Omnipotent. Jesus said, "All power is given unto me in heaven and in earth" (Matt.28:18b).
4. God is Omniscient. No thought, plan, purpose, or secret of man is hidden from God. Even the names and numbers of stars are known to Him. He is never surprised at what happens.
5. God is holiness personified. He is justice and mercy combined. He is the essence of love.

He is all this and much more. To the Christian, He is Savior, Lord, Master, Father, protector, provider, shepherd, guide, lover, comforter, enabler, and coming King.

How can anyone refuse to serve a God like that?

Angels
Heb. 1:14

The average person says that there is the possibility that angels exist. But it is so unreal and so fantastic that few have wanted to give the subject much serious thought. Yet the Bible contains more than 300 references where angels were commissioned to come from heaven to earth on some kind of business for God.

The word *angel* is a name signifying literally a messenger or a person sent. Sometimes it denotes a human being, but it most often refers to invisible, created heavenly hosts. It is used in the Book of Revelation to speak of the bishops or pastors of the seven churches.

Who are these angels?

1. They are not glorified saints. Yet they are holy beings. They were never people.
2. They were made before man was created, even before earth was created (Job 38:7).
3. They are not all-wise (Matt.24:36).
4. They are not to be worshipped (Rev. 22:8).
5. They rejoice in the salvation of souls on earth (Luke 15:7).
6. They have names.
7. They are not all equal. There are angels, archangels, seraphim, and cherubim.
8. They are beings of great activity and strength. Each angel has his own work to do.
9. They are interested in our temporal lives. For example, Hagar, Lot, Isaac, as well as our home life.
10. They protect us from dangers. For example, the three Hebrew children, Daniel, Peter, and Paul.

11. They are God's reapers (Matt. 24:31).
12. They are our unseen guests (Heb.13:2).
13. They will accompany Jesus when He returns to earth (Matt. 25:11; I Thess. 4).
14. They are not all-powerful.

Miracles
Acts 2:22

If we should eliminate the miraculous from the religion of Jesus Christ, we would face greater problems than the miracles themselves.

If you take from the Bible and from Christianity every element of the miraculous, you will soon discover that you have so torn the garment of faith that it is no longer useful.

The Bible is a miraculous Book containing records of numerous miracles. Its authorship is miraculous, its preservation is as miraculous, and centuries have been witness to its miraculous power to change lives and nations.

Two basic miracles in the Old Testament and the New are the birth of Isaac and the birth of Jesus. God did something that nature, of her own power could not do.

I. Jesus pointed to the miracles He performed as proof of His Messiahship (Matt 11:2-4; 20-24). Yet people had not repented because of His mighty works.

II. Miracles are God's unusual method of working. He ordinarily operates according to that which we call natural laws. In reality no more of God's power is displayed in His unusual workings than in His normal procedure. It is only a different display of power.

   The feeding of the 5,000 by multiplying the loaves and fishes took no more power than to feed the billions of people of earth every day. It seems to be a matter of demand and supply. He faced the need; He was the source of supply.

III. There is no contradiction of natural law in a miracle, merely the substituting of lower laws for higher ones. This happens every day. For example, the skyscrapers in a city or airplanes in the sky.

If man can supersede gravitation by interposing the operation of other forces, shall we deny God's ability to supersede any law of nature as He pleases?

In the Old Testament we find more than 50 miracles; in the New Testament some 40 miracles are recorded. Most were for some benefit. Two—the withered fig tree and the destruction of a large number of hogs—had adverse effects.

A. Old Testament miracles can be divided into 3 classes:

1. Miracles of judgment of God upon disobedient nations.
2. Miracles which witness to God's favor upon Israel. For example, the plagues of Egypt.
3. Miracles that witness to God's power before Israel. For example, Elijah on Mt. Carmel.

B. In the New Testament Jesus' miracles may be divided into four classes:

1. The power of Jesus over nature,
2. His power over demons,
3. His power over disease,
4. His power over death.

The miracles of Christ were purposeful, constructive, and elevating.

Jesus often taught a spiritual lesson along with His miracle of healing.

IV. The first miracle of Jesus shows us the purpose in all His miracles (John 2). This first miracle was one of supply and it demonstrated that Jesus brings joy. This joy of the

Lord will have its full manifestation at the Marriage Supper of the Lamb.
V. For long periods of time past no miracles are recorded. For example, from Eden to the flood; 400 years in Egypt; 450 years before the birth of Christ.

A Look at Jesus

It is surprising that we do not know more about Jesus and that we do not know Him better when His image is so clearly portrayed for us in the four gospels.

The pictures we have of Him have been in the world more than 2000 years. Through all that period nothing has been added and nothing has really been taken away.

Had you lived in the first century you would most likely have been among those who saw in Jesus nothing but a disturber of the peace. But those who knew Him best, the gospel writers, knew otherwise.

I. Notice how His heart went out to those who suffered.
Physical distress wrung His heart. Sickness in the first century did not receive much attention. People considered it a result of sin. The poor suffered unattended. There were no hospitals. Insane people were not housed and cared for. No one else reached out a helping hand, but Jesus pitied them.

No doubt hordes of worshipers on the way to the Temple passed the paralytic at the pool over a period of 38 years and paid no attention to him. Maybe someone tossed him a coin occasionally. Then Jesus came!

"Do you want to be made whole?" Jesus asked. From that day on, the man was whole.

If any man in Palestine was shunned more than a maniac, it was a leper. But neither was beyond the reach of His heart.

II. Jesus was always interested in the neglected and forlorn.
The Samaritans were outcasts, but they were human, so Jesus befriended them. He not only passed through

Samaria—when most Jews avoided it entirely—but He encountered the woman at the well and won her as a disciple and a witness.

III. Outcasts even in Galilee and Judea, estranged from organized religion and branded as "sinners" by the very religious, found a friend in Jesus. These were people who had no use for religious ceremonies, who took no interest in the Rabbis or their teachings. Thus the Rabbis took no interest in them.

Religious leaders pronounced a ban on them. No Rabbi would mingle with such people or risk his good name by dining with one of them. But Jesus went home with them and ate with them. The Pharisees never forgave Him for that.

Among the so-called "sinners" was a group lower than all the others. They were called "Publicans." They were tax collectors whose business was to collect Jewish money and send it to Rome. They were considered lower than dogs. The Jewish leaders would not even allow them to contribute to their treasury.

Yet Jesus made friends with these men. One was Matthew; another was Zachaeus.

IV. In His attitude toward women, what a difference Jesus made! In the Arab world, women have always been considered inferior to men. Sometimes woman has been a toy, more frequently a slave, but invariably a little higher than an animal.

A woman's position in Palestine was above that of women in surrounding nations, but even there, she was at the mercy of the man.

But when the woman taken in adultery was brought before Him, Jesus didn't hesitate to defend the rights of women. He challenged the men who brought her to Him. He knew they were as guilty as she. When Jesus said, "Let him who is without sin cast the first stone," they couldn't get away fast enough.

Jesus' encounter with the Samaritan woman at the well

amazed His disciples who had gone into the city to buy food. Yet Jesus considered her as any other lost soul who needed His help.

V. Jesus loved people. He loved a crowd. The masses were dear to His heart. His invitations were always generous.

VI. Jesus changed people. He changed their habits and opinions and ambitions. He changed their tempers and dispositions and natures. They were never the same after they met Him. Wherever He went He transformed lives. And what He did in Palestine, He has been doing ever since.

VII. Some men are great in their influence for a generation. On the contrary, Jesus is a living reality today! And He has promised to come back to receive His own.

CHAPTER 6

Thoughts on Prayer

Prayer is

1. The language of love between Father and Son, accompanied by strength and self-acceptance.
2. The language of obedience between Master and disciple. We cannot coerce God to bend His will to do things our way.
3. The language of mercy between giver and intercessor.

When we pray, instead of asking, "What wilt Thou have me to do?" we often say, "This is what I'd like to do." And we want to get God's approval of our desires.

We should never rise from our knees without a wandering thanksgiving that God has borne with us at all—He being what He is, and we being what we are.

When asking for God's guidance, it is difficult to put self and our consideration of self out of the reckoning.

Times of meeting with God are like clearings in a jungle. We can see the eternal stars again and feel the winds of God cool upon our hot faces.

Prayer is a person-to-God encounter. Real prayer is a meeting of heaven and earth.

God *does* answer prayer. When a believer talks to God and gets no answer, there's a reason. James said, "You have not because you ask not." He adds that we don't always get what we want because we "ask amiss" for selfish reasons.

Before we can pray with much depth or meaning, we should consider three basic facts:

1. We must believe in God, the Father, maker of heaven and earth.
2. We must believe that God cares, that He is concerned for our welfare, and that He wants the best for us. If it matters to us, it matters to Him.
3. We must want strength, above all else, to do His will as it is revealed to us.

When you pray

1. Look at yourself. God sees the pray-er before He listens to the prayer itself.
2. Look at your motive. Why should God give you a raise in salary? Perhaps if He did it would mean your stealing more from Him. Ask the question, my will or His?
3. Don't give up easily. God may have a different answer to your prayer from what you expect. His answer may be delayed. And sometimes unanswered prayers bring greater blessings. Trust God's wisdom. "Seek first the kingdom of God and His righteousness."

Prayer is the greatest power in this world. It's a pity we don't make greater use of it.

To realize that God is only a prayer away is one of the most important discoveries we can make.

Spiritual power will always vary in direct proportion to spiritual dedication.

Everything depends upon whether in prayer we are trying to *change* the will of God or to *find* the will of God; to make use of God or to let Him use us.

Prayer is never ours to alter or change God's will, but to ascertain it.

Many a prayer is answered, but we're often too dull to recognize the answer when it comes.

Some people look upon prayer as a last resort to get help when everything else has failed.

When we pray we are ushered into the Throne Room for an audience with the King of the universe for an indefinite time.

If we are going to receive from God, we must be willing to accept what He has to give, and to receive it on His terms, not ours.

If you pray for money so that you can live in luxury and abundance,

If you ask God for brains so that you can live by exploiting your fellow man,

If you want success because your vanity demands applause,"

Don't expect an answer to any such selfish prayers.

Some of us spend our whole lives saying, "Lord, help me do what I want to do."

We need faith to carry us on when the church service is over and we are face to face with the daily grind of making a living.

We need faith to hold us steady when we walk through deep valleys and dark days, when discouragement dogs our footsteps and we are tempted to give up the struggle, when perfection doesn't seem so perfect, and the divine is clouded by the human.

There is nothing mysterious about faith. It underlies all of life.

One of the greatest gifts of God to man is the capacity to pray. Why is it that for all our talk about prayer, so many of us don't make it a part of our everyday living?

There are some explanations, of course:

1. We live such crowded lives today that some things have to be left out.
2. We have so much confidence in our human ingenuity that prayer is not as necessary as people once thought. We have the doctor, the wonder drug prescriptions and such.
3. Some of us have had some bad experiences with prayer. We prayed and prayed and nothing happened, so gradually we gave it up.

"When you pray, say 'Our Father. . . . '"It is not a child's prayer. It is for the disciples, the model for all people and for all ages.

"Our Father." There is no evidence that any people ever considered themselves the children of God until after Jesus came. In the Old Testament, God is set forth as a father only four times.

"Hallowed be thy name." In that "brief, grand prayer," as Thomas Carlisle called it, there are 7 sections. This one has to be answered by the one who prays. We best hallow His name by lives of holiness and purity.

"Thy kingdom come." The kingdom is a spiritual brotherhood of redeemed people.

"Thy will be done." We measure God's goodness by the extent to which we are spared pain and trouble. But God's purpose is to conform us to the image of His Son, and His Son died on a cross. To conform us to His image and to save us from trouble, even great trouble, are two contradictory things that can't be reconciled.

Had I been in Jerusalem during those hours in which Christ was betrayed, tried, and retried, condemned and led to Calvary, I would have prayed earnestly that God would intervene before it was too late, and for His kingdom's sake. But had that prayer of mine been heard and granted, where would our poor, desperate world be today?

It is only 70 words long, but grand beyond any speech other than its own. Here is one prayer which every Christian can engage in. It is the most private, the most public, the most practical of all prayers. It is as high as the sky, as wide as the world, and equal to all our needs and longings.

It is a fact that most Americans pray. The will to pray is almost instinctive. But with many, prayer is spasmodic and occasional. To some, it is meaningless.

1. Prayer is not a mechanism by which we get an immediate and automatic response from God.
2. Prayer is not primarily a way of getting things from God.
3. Prayer is really simple; it takes no special skill
4. Prayer does not necessarily have to be spoken aloud.
5. Prayer is blasphemy if it does not alter your life.

Our true prayers are the desires that dominate our lives.

Prayer is simply talking with our Heavenly Father. For example, a father who had four children. The first, a small boy, came to ask, "Daddy, may I have a quarter for ice cream?" The 7-year-old daughter came to her daddy in tears. She had skinned her arm while playing. "Daddy, kiss the pain away," she cried. He did.

The third one, a girl in her early teens, came to him with homework. He helped her solve her problem.

The fourth climbed up into his daddy's lap. "I really don't want anything," he said. "I just want to be with you."

We can come to our Heavenly Father with all our needs: material things, healing when we bump up against rough places and hurt, or solutions to problems we can't solve in our own wisdom. But some of the most rewarding prayer times are when we just tell Him how much we love Him.

A professional man was having domestic problems and, as a result, was drinking too much. He went to his pastor.

"Do you ever pray?" the pastor asked.

"Yes, of course I pray!" he said.

"What do you do and what do you say when you pray?"

"Oh, I tell God over and over just exactly what I want and what I want Him to do."

Then the pastor asked, "Did it ever occur to you that sometime God might ask you, 'Which of us is God? Are you telling me, or am I telling you?'"

Sometimes the answer to prayer is delayed for the general good. For example, if I ask God to make His Son Jesus Christ the world's universal king, I haven't considered the consequences. If God were to do that—if He should answer that prayer now—He would have to kill every sinner in the world, cut short their probation period, remove all possibility and probability of repentance and send them immediately to hell. God, in His goodness, is doing all He can to see men repent and turn to Him.

True prayer is connecting yourself up with the unseen environment charged with creative power. Down this connecting line of prayer the infinite resources and energies of that unseen world are flowing into your life so that you are able to face the hardest task or the most difficult situation with the knowledge of God's adequacy and His inexhaustibility.

When we pray we must always remember three things:

1. The love of God, which desires only what is best for us;
2. The wisdom of God, which alone knows what is best for us;
3. The power of God, which alone can bring to pass that which is best for us.

1. Prayer sets things in their proper perspective.
2. Prayer achieves release from anxiety by bringing our wills into harmony with God's will.
3. Prayer offers release from anxiety by liberating within us new resources of power for handling the difficult business of living.
4. Prayer is the divine in us appealing to the Divine above us. Praise is to be the keynote—the beginning, the middle, and the end of every prayer.

C.S. Dodd said, "We cannot know our real needs or grasp God's plan. So actually all we can bring to God is an inarticulate sigh which the Spirit will translate to God for us."

1. Prayer recognizes the true relation existing between God and man.
2. Prayer prevents one from forgetting God.
3. Prayer activates spiritual desires.
4. Prayer adjusts man's feeling in harmony with his fellow man, as well as with God.
5. True prayer is always answered: "Yes," "No," or "Wait."

Jesus prayed three times in Gethsemane. This was more than shrinking of the flesh at the thought of dying. It was more than human suffering.

Had that prayer been answered, there never would have been a Calvary. There never would have been the great songs like "When I Survey the Wondrous Cross."

I believe that God yearned to grant that prayer, just as He wants to grant our prayers.

I hope I'm not irreverent to think and to say that today, in glory, the Savior thanks His Father that the thrice-repeated prayer was refused.

God so loved the world and was so anxious for its redemption that the cry of His well beloved Son was refused.

We read of healings in the Bible. We witness them among others. And yet our own bodies, or those of our relatives swell with disease. Where is God? Why won't He answer?

In the Bible, the son of a widow of Nain was restored, but there were other sons who died. Peter was set free from prison, but John the Baptist was beheaded. Paul was used to heal people, but his own request for healing was denied.

Here again we're reminded of Jesus' prayer in Gethsemane, "Nevertheless, not as I will, but as Thou wilt."

God is always listening. But prayer must be in accordance with His will.

1. Obedience is the condition for prayer.
2. Abiding in Christ is a prerequisite.
3. Prayer must be in His name.

When we pray we link ourselves with the inexhaustible motive power that spins the universe and we are asking that a part of that great power be apportioned to our needs.

Prayer is an attitude of the soul before it is a petition on your lips.

When we pray we cease to carry on alone.

CHAPTER 7

Insights into the Word

How Jesus Worked

Jesus had no special technique that He used twice. But he always got the attention of a person fixed upon His own personality. He never dealt the same with any two people. How different from the way we try to bring people to Him in our day!

Jesus came through the throng one day and saw Zachaeus sitting in a sycamore tree. He said to him, "Zachaeus, come down!" And the little man slid down the sycamore tree and into the kingdom of God. He must have been in the kingdom when he hit the ground, because as soon as he got his breath, he said, "The half of my goods I give to the poor, and those whom I've wronged, I will repay four-fold." It would take more than the jolt of sliding down a sycamore tree trunk to get a Jewish IRS agent to do that.

If only some of us had been there. We would have capitalized on the incident. We could have organized a church—The Church of the Sycamore Sliders. In all our sanctuaries we would have planted a sycamore tree. At first the trees would have been the natural crude sycamores. But as time went on, and as the movement grew, we would have made the tree easier to slide down.

Oh, to be sure, we would have preached that no one could ever get into the kingdom unless he slid down the sycamore tree as did Zachaeus, our founder. We would no doubt remove the knots and rough bark. Finally we would pad the tree and then shorten the slide. Some congregations would use a polished, gently inclined slide, and people might even have a little car with ball bearing rollers, so they could gently slide into the Kingdom.

Older members would sadly shake their heads and say, "When I slid down, the bark was on the tree and there were knots on it. We did it right in those days. It looks like our church is going to the dogs." No knots, no religion.

Strange, but the statement Zachaeus made about restitution would be overlooked. The whole emphasis would be on the sycamore tree.

But we have no record that Jesus ever said to another person, "Come down."

Or take the case of Nicodemus who came to Jesus by night. The Bible doesn't say, but everyone believes he carried a lantern. Somewhere I saw a picture of him as he came to Jesus, carrying a lantern.

If this had happened in our generation, someone would have stressed the lantern. He might have started The Church of the Lantern, using a lantern as its symbol. The secular world might have called them "Lanternites."

No matter where they held services, all members would be required to carry a lantern, even in the daylight. In time, they would discontinue carrying lanterns and wear lantern pins, put up lantern posters, and display lantern banners.

It would be a great lantern movement. Books would be written about the causes that led to Nicodemus' choice of that certain kind of lantern. A lot of controversy would arise over the actual time he lit the lantern that night. Some would say at nine o'clock; scholars equally as prominent would go to great lengths to prove it was eight-fifty-nine.

During this emphasis on the lantern and the controversy over the time Nicodemus lit the lantern, it would be easy to forget that Jesus said to Nicodemus, "You must be born again."

This seems to be the only time Jesus said, "Ye must be born

again." As important as the new birth is, Jesus used that expression only once, as far as we know. The important thing was getting that man's attention centered on Jesus and what He commanded.

The living, radiant presence of Christ! That is what we need most to bring people to Him. That is really all we need.

We are not told that Jesus opened the meetings of His little flock with prayer. Strange, but he didn't take an offering either. Of course we need offerings. But we have no record that Jesus had Judas to pass the plate every time they met.

We're not told that Jesus invited them to an altar of prayer while they sang an invitation hymn at the close of His message. {I'm not saying anything against that method; but evidently Jesus didn't do it that way}. Nor are we told that He passed out decision cards.

We can often make a mistake in our emphasis upon an experience. No experience ever satisfies the human heart. If we have Him in all of His fullness, we will have His gifts of the new birth, His purity, and His power. We come short, however, if we do not emphasize His living, abiding, glorious presence.

How the Church Came Down Through the Ages

The church sprang into being in a day's time, when on the Day of Pentecost the Holy Spirit transformed the weak and fearful disciples into the bold and powerful exponents of the Lord Jesus Christ who witnessed with power everywhere to everybody.

The history of the church is divided into several periods:

I. The Apostolic Period (c. 30-100)
II. The Persecution Period (100-331)

    A. Persecution in Jerusalem (Acts 8:1). Christians scattered
    B. Nero—the burning of Rome (65-68)
    C. Emperor Domitian (90-96)
    D. Roman Emperors Trajan and Adrian (108-138)
    E. Marcus Aurelius (162-179) Polycarp and his disciples martyred

F. Decius (249-253) more intense persecution
G. Valerian (257) met a terrible death and persecution himself
H. Diocletian (303-313) a determined effort to destroy Christianity

III. Constantine came to power in 313
Churches organized into units, headed by bishops. In a short while nearly half the people in the empire called themselves Christians.

IV. The Established Period (313-590)
Constantine had issued his edict of toleration. In 325 he founded a new city. In 476, Rome fell. About 405, there were images and martyrs in the church.

V. The Dark Ages (590-1216)

A. The rise of Mohammedanism (732), the Battle of Tours. Charles Martel drove the Moslems back into Spain and later to Africa.
B. Two factions of the Church—Eastern and Western—emerged.
In 1054 the Pope of Rome excommunicated the Patriarch of Constantinople. In 1066 the churches divided.
C. The Crusades were from 1095-1455.

VI. The Pre-Reformation Period (1216-1455)
The Lollards, John Hus, Savonarola
VII. The Reformation Period (1455-1792)
Discovery of printing. Martin Luther. The Jesuits (1534)
VIII. The Modern Period (1792-Present time)
Missionary movements

Man

The New Testament has six things to say in particular about man:

1. It says that man is a child of God by creation, but he has forfeited his place in the divine family by his own willful disobedience, and he must now have a Father's forgiveness to regain his former place.
2. It says that man has lost his way in the journey of life and will never find it again unless a Guide comes from heaven to help him.
3. It says that man is sick—desperately sick—of soul and that he must have a Divine Physician who admits no incurable cases, to cure him of the deadly disease of sin.
4. It says that man is tempted, overwhelmed by his temptation, and must have a Divine Helper to give him strength with which to conquer and master his sin.
5. It says that man is a servant, but that he is now serving the wrong master, and he must be converted in order to give his allegiance to a new Master, Christ.
6. It says that man is a prisoner, a prisoner of evil habits, and that he must have a Liberator, a Redeemer, a Savior, who can cancel his past sins and open the doors of his prison and bring him out into new light.

Names, Applications, and Titles Given to Jesus

The Advocate
The Almighty
The Alpha and Omega
The Amen
The Author and Finisher of Our Faith
The Bread of Life
The Carpenter
The Chief Corner Stone
The Christ
The Counselor
The Deliverer
The Door
The Fountain

The Gate
The Gift of God
The Governor
The Good Shepherd
The Great Physician
The Horn of Salvation
The I Am
Immanuel—God With Us
The Son of the Living God
King of Kings
The Lamb
The Life
The Light
The Lion of the Tribe of Judah
The Man
The Mediator
The Messenger of the Covenant
The Messiah
The Morning Star
The Nazarene
The Only Begotten of the Father
The Priest
The Prince of Peace
The Prophet
The Propitiation
The Ransom
The Redeemer
The Resurrection and the Life
The Rock
The Rose of Sharon
The Savior
The Shield
The Son of David
The Son of Man
The Sun of Righteousness
The Teacher

The Truth
The Vine
The Way
The Witness

Bible scholars say there are about 250 names given to Jesus Christ throughout Scripture. These are the best known.

Pivotal Events of the Old Testament:

1. The creation and fall of man
2. The flood
3. The call of Abraham
    From Genesis 12 onward, we are concerned with one man and his descendants.
4. The Egyptian interlude
5. The call of Moses
6. The Exodus—God's deliverance of His people from bondage
7. The wilderness wanderings—the Tabernacle, sacrifices
8. The conquest of Canaan
9. The rise of the kingdom—the Temple built
10. The divided kingdom
11. The fall of Israel
12. The fall of Judah
13. The exile—God's people carried away into captivity
14. The restoration—Jerusalem and the temple rebuilt
15. The coming of Messiah—Christ

The Gospel of Christ

This gospel is the only Gospel, the one and only source of salvation, the only way to heaven. Today, of course, it is popular to be broad and liberal in matters of religion. But have you ever stopped to realize that people hardly appreciate broadness or liberality in other professions?

How many of you would respect a physician who leads a

sick man to a medicine cabinet, and, instead of offering him the one remedy that could cure him says, "Take anything you want! These are all good for something"?

What would you think of an attorney who rejects the one and only clear way to win your case, and, instead points you to a library of law books, saying, "Choose any of these records: These cases were all conducted by eminent lawyers and contain interesting points of procedure"?

What about the preacher who proclaims from his pulpit, "Here are all the religions of the world, choose whatever one you want. They all have something good in them,"? Yet Christ Himself emphatically declared "I am the Way, the Truth, and the Life . . . ."

Then why listen to clergymen who say that the *Koran*, the *Talmud*, or the so-called "Sacred Books of the East" are placed side by side with the Bible, even though the Scripture tells us "There is none other name under heaven given among men whereby we must be saved," but the holy, precious name of Jesus?

How long would you employ a guide in the great Northern woods who would suggest, "Take any trail you want. They all lead somewhere"?

Why then risk your immortal soul by following the popular teacher who would try to tell us that all men, Christian and pagan, Gentile and Jew, Trinitarian and Unitarian, Modernist or Fundamentalist—all are taking different roads to the same final goal.

Call me narrow, one-sided, intolerant if you will. But there is one Mediator between God and man, Jesus Christ, one gospel, one faith, one heaven.

Salvation is not something you take or leave without affecting your soul. Jesus says, "Ye must be born again." If you want your Savior's guidance, love, and help; if on the great day of resurrection, you hope to see your Savior face to face and spend eternity with Him; if you want to sing with assurance, "Heaven is my home," then you must be born again.

It is not enough to be a nominal church member Some

unbelievers cover their disloyalty with a pious front, and many Christ-denying congregations have failed to lead their members to salvation.

It is not sufficient that you are an honored and distinguished citizen in your community. Public acclaim never opens the doors of paradise.

You cannot be satisfied with claiming that you are sincere in your religion. The Indians who burn their eyes out by gazing into the blazing sun are sincere. But they are mistaken. You must do more than contribute money, sing in church choirs, or occupy congregational offices. You must be born again. It is not enough that you have been confirmed and have made a public declaration of your faith; thousands who have done all that are now unfaithful.

The Gospel of Christ demands that we accept Him as Lord, be born again, and live according to His teachings.

CHAPTER 8

Red Flag Alert

"Put on the whole armour of God, that ye may be able to stand against the wiles of the devil" (Eph. 6:1).

Paul's letters to Timothy are How-To books for his son in the faith. He urges this young preacher to "Fight the good fight of faith." Can you imagine any preacher's mentor's telling his student to fight? And, of all things, Paul says, "I have fought a good fight" (II Tim.4:7).

What does Paul mean "fight"? Didn't he know that a Christian is not supposed to fight? Yet even as a Christian, Paul contended for his faith, sometimes at fearful cost.

Not only did the early Christians need Paul's admonition, we need it today. Living for Christ and sharing His teachings inevitably brings conflict.

Consider the martyrs, whose blood became the seed of the church. Christians around the globe continue to suffer and die for their faith. We Americans have not yet been subjected to torture or death for our faith. Who knows when we will be, though our enemies would destroy our faith by more subtle means.

As I write, a battle rages in Oklahoma City over whether gays and lesbians have a right to fly banners on city light poles. They already have their filthy messages plastered on park benches around town.

State by state they fight to coerce voters and win the right to "same-sex marriages"—a total contradiction of terms. They have had remarkable success.

They even had the audacity to attack the Boy Scouts of America, demanding that homosexual Scout leaders be accepted.

Teachers in some states are required to teach homosexuality as an acceptable lifestyle.

Abortion rights advocates have made the most dangerous place for a baby its mother's womb.

Our Supreme Court bans prayer, Bible study, and reference to God in public schools. Instead, children are subjected to teachings contrary to God's Word. Darwin's theory is taught as fact—though Darwin repudiated it in later life. But the fact of divine creation is denounced.

Students are taught—often by example—that sex outside of marriage is not only permissible, but also desirable. In a community college where I taught, several faculty members had affairs and divorced their mates one year. Illicit sex, illegal drugs, firearms, and violence run rampant in our schools.

Instead of a sanctity for peace, decency, and safety, home has become one of bitterness, adultery, child abuse, and abortion.

With the aid of the news media and the internet, our society is fast becoming as decadent as the Roman Empire.

But a decadent society is not all Christians must fight. We must fight to defend the faith.

Not only did Jesus warn against false prophets (Matt. 7:19), but Peter issues a similar warning, describing some of their ways: " . . . . and through covetousness shall they with feigned words make merchandise of you" (II Peter 2:1, 3).

Despite these and other specific cautions, most of us hesitate to question anyone's religious beliefs and practices, especially if they include a few scripture references.

At all costs, we don't want to be called intolerant. So the deception thrives on our indifference.

Wolves on the Prowl

Jesus likens false prophets and teachers to wolves. That metaphor fits perfectly with His metaphor of the Good Shepherd and His sheep.

I wouldn't call anyone a wolf, but, reading the following letter, I "smelled a rat," as you can judge from my comments in brackets.

These excerpts were taken from a letter written to a friend of mine—and probably sent to thousands. It's a perfect example of the tactics of those Peter describes. Greed is evident throughout. The writer uses every psychological gimmick imaginable to get money from this elderly recipient.

1. Uses the first name again and again
2. "Not everybody is even going to receive this letter."
3. "God meant it for you."
4. "Something SUPERNATURAL the Lord wants to do for you!"
5. "The Holy Spirit has been speaking to me about ministering to you and praying for you in a very specific way . . . and He very clearly impressed it upon my heart to send this message to you."
6. "This is not a gimmick. [If it isn't I'd like to know what a gimmick is].
    This is very serious business." {That's the truth!]
7. "This letter has been birthed from the heart of God. A clear word from the Lord." [Wow! Inspired no less!]
8. "This is one of those kinds of MIRACLE MINISTRY MOMENTS."
9. "Are you facing a financial famine?" [Who isn't?]
10. "DO YOU NEED A MIRACLE OF MULTIPLICATION IN YOUR FINANCES?
11. "I've never been more serious."
12. "God wants to do something for you and I don't want you to miss it. PLEASE KEEP READING."

13. (recipient's name)—"It's time for your MIRACLE OF MULTIPLICATION! That's the message the Lord wanted me to send you today."
14. "HE SPOKE TO MY HEART—to encourage you to . . . follow the EXAMPLE of the BOY with the LUNCH! He gave what he had."
15. This is BIBLE—and if it's BIBLE, it is GOD."
16. "It's time for you to see whether His Word will come true for you or not. It's time to take what little you have left and GET THOSE DEBTS PAID IN FULL."
17. "Here's all you need to do: Go to the last page of this letter and let us know WHERE you need your MIRACLE of MULTIPLICATION. TAKE WHAT YOU HAVE . . . and GIVE IT TO JESUS. SEND THIS ENTIRE LETTER BACK." {Why do they want this *entire* letter back? Obviously they don't want a skeptic like me to get hold of it}.
18. "IN FACT, we have had meetings over this letter . . . and literally saturated this simple letter with volumes of prayer already. We want God to use it as a ministry tool to touch your life like never before."
19. Prayer: Eph. 3:20
    "Dear heavenly Father,
    "I thank You that You do exceedingly above all that we can ask or think, when we sow in Your kingdom . . . feeding people all around the world because this ministry is so blessed with multiplication.
    "And I thank You, Lord, that everyone who sows will have the most delicious lunch they have ever had. I thank You for each one and their commitment to sow into Your kingdom . . . Amen."

20. "If what you've got is not enough to meet your need then give it to Jesus to transform into your miracle, limitless supply."
21. "I don't often say this . . . but you may need to take this more seriously than you've ever taken a ministry letter from me before.

LET THE HOLY SPIRIT ... show you the amount that represents your ... LUNCH OFFERING of faith."
22. "He may tell you to empty your pockets. You may need to clear out an old checking account or crack a piggy bank.... He'd like you to ... release your faith for your miracle of multiplication."
23. "Say, YES to God's leading and RUSH your 'brown bag lunch' offering into the work of the Lord today."
{Now for the clincher}:

P.S. BEGIN RIGHT NOW—TURN THIS PAGE OVER and let us know where you need a MIRACLE of MULTIPLICATION in your life. SEND THIS ENTIRE LETTER BACK in the enclosed pre-addressed envelope."
{Note that word *entire* again}.

"MIRACLE OF MULTIPLICATION
PERSONAL PRAYER PAGE

Dear _____ and the entire Prayer Ministry Team,

This is _____ from _____ _____, and YES—I'm ready for a "Miracle of Multiplication" in my life!

This is the NUMBER ONE area(s) where I'm asking you to believe God with me for a bountiful, supernatural, overflowing "MIRACLE of MULTIPLICATION" IN MY LIFE.
_____
_____

Here are some HEAVY CARES and CONCERNS that I don't want to CARRY anymore. Please join me in CASTING these CARES over to the Lord ... for Him to deal with.
_____
_____
_____

I have a LOVED ONE who needs a "Miracle of Multiplication" and "Divine Intervention" from God. The FIRST NAME of this loved one is _____.

Please pray for the following for this person _____
_____
_____
_____

YES—I believe when I invest in God's kingdom, there is always an overflow! . . . I sow . . . in His name into the ministry to help feed the multitudes with His Word.

The amount of my "Miracle of Multiplication" gift is $_____. I ALSO want to sow a PROXY SEED for a LOVED ONE who has a MIRACLE NEED. In Jesus' name I'm sowing $_____ on their behalf. I have a SPECIAL HEART for MISSIONS and I'm enclosing a WORLD OUTREACH MISSIONS/Ministry GIFT of $_____ for you to use wherever the needs are greatest in your outreach.

Please make your checks payable to:
_____
_____
_____"

My godly, conscientious friend had his letter filled out and his check written. But before he mailed it he decided to consult me. I saved him a few hundred dollars which he told me he needed for that month's living expenses.

The following excerpt is from a letter I received recently from another TV evangelist. It takes a very different approach.

"We have stated over and over again that the elderly, widows who are barely able to survive, and the unemployed need not send us any money.

"My daily prayer is, 'Oh, God, help us never to waste or misspend any gift from the elderly or needy.'

"Please—once again—may I remind all our elderly friends: Please do not send us money that you need to live on. Just pray for us . . . . And please do not respond to any appeal for money from any evangelist or ministry that pressures you or makes you feel guilty for not helping them. Any ministry that will take your food or rent money and leave you in dire need is not of God. Your local church comes first."

If I had more money to give than my local church needs for its ministries, you can guess which of these two I would support.

No reputable minister would ask someone to crack a piggy bank in hopes of buying a miracle. Miracles are not for sale.

I'd rather stand before God at the Judgment and face the charge of robbing a bank with a gun than to face the charge of using scripture to seduce anyone to crack a piggy bank so I could live in a mansion with gold bathroom fixtures, wear mink coats, and drive Rolls Royces.

Even Satan can quote scripture. He tried that on Jesus.

Jim Bakker reportedly said, "As long as people are stupid enough to send me money. I'll take it." And his sin found him out. So will that of others. But, unfortunately, not before they have fleeced a lot of God's conscientious children out of their money.

In his letter to Timothy, Paul warns: "But evil men and seducers shall wax worse and worse, deceiving and being deceived" (II Tim. 3:13). He says that in the latter times, "some shall depart from the faith, giving heed to seducing spirits, and doctrines of devils; Speaking lies in hypocrisy; having their conscience seared with a hot iron" (I Tim. 4:1-2).

Jesus said, "For there shall arise false Christs, and false prophets, and shall show great signs and wonders; insomuch that, if it were possible, they shall deceive the very elect" (Matt.24:24).

False prophets and teachers prey on the most vulnerable—often the elderly, the conscientious, and the poor. Some may be vulnerable because of their own greed. They're led to believe that miracles are for sale. "Send us money and we'll pray for you" is a favorite ploy.

Those who major on healing or financial prosperity instead of on salvation with Jesus as its only source are false teachers regardless of how much scripture they quote.

Some have interpreted John's greeting to his friend Gaius (III John 1:2) to mean that God wants everyone to prosper. Even that God wishes *"above all else"* that we prosper—financially of course—and be in good health. God didn't say that, John did. It's as if I wrote to a friend and said, "I hope you stay well and win the lottery." One TV evangelist wrote a book based on his interpretation of John's words and no doubt helped make his own fortune at the expense of gullible listeners.

Jesus had more to say about man and his relationship to money than about almost any other subject. He said, "It is easier for a camel to go through the eye of a needle than for a rich man to enter the kingdom of God" (Mark 10:23). He said the beggar Lazarus went to Paradise; the rich man Dives went to hell.

That doesn't mean a rich man can't get to heaven. It means that he must make money legitimately, invest it wisely, and use it to further God's kingdom—not to line some false teacher's pocket.

God promises to supply all our needs and in the Sermon on the Mount Jesus warns us not to be too concerned over material things. Paul tells Timothy that the "love of money is the root of all evil" (I Tim. 6:10).

By using selected scriptural passages, we can "prove" almost anything from the Bible. If we are seeking the truth, however, we need to follow the general teachings of the Word. They point us to Jesus, our one and only Savior, who not only saves us but supplies all our needs—physical, financial, and spiritual. That truth we can trust. For that faith, we can live or die.

An Introduction to the Cults

The greatest challenge to Christianity today is not atheism but false religions.

Cults by the hundreds that were unknown a few years ago have sprung up overnight. They represent a break with the mainstream of religious tradition of the society in which they exist.

It is estimated that there are more than 5,000 religious and pseudo-religious cults in the USA. These cults are flourishing and accelerating in spite of the terrible fate that overtook the followers of Jim Jones.

"I would say that there are 30 million Americans involved in Eastern cults," a former Indian guru said, "and I wonder what conditions will be like in ten or fifteen years if this trend is not reversed."

Most cults draw their recruits from the 17 to 25 age bracket. In the United States alone, cults involve millions of young adults as members.

Why do they attract young people?

1. They seek to have real needs fulfilled. For example, they take advantage of youth rebellion.
2. They convey a sense of family in that youth are cared for, accepted, loved, fed, and made to feel important.
3. There is a sense of community.
4. Many young people are down on their luck when first approached. California is the end of the line.
5. Some are merely curious or spiritually hungry, or both.

Why the explosion of cults on the American scene at this time in history? Is their emergence in recent years a sociological sign of the times, or is it a spiritual indicator of the times? It's probably both.

What can we do?

1. High school and college youths must be informed about the cults and how they operate.
2. Without endangering other rights, we can, and we must, enact legislation which will discourage deception and fraud in fund raising and recruitment by cults.
3. We must create and support groups which practice sensitive, tender, and loving rehabilitation of cult victims.
4. Christians and Christian churches must get their act together

by trying to meet the spiritual needs of young people especially.

The thrust of the new religious groups—Eastern mystical, occult, or aberrant Christian—is that experience is more important than doctrine, and feeling is more important than rationality.

Many young Americans during the decade of the 60's were leading lives of ease and emptiness. Disenchanted with the establishment and disillusioned by the failure of politics and caught up in the drug culture, they were ready for the emergence of new religious movements.

"Our modern religious cults," says Dr. Paul S. Rees, "for the most part, are only ancient heresies wearing a new dress."

Each cult is headed by a self-proclaimed prophet who claims to have new revelations.

1. Cult leaders exercise power over their people. They require total obedience, submission, subjection.
2. They are in it for the money it affords. Like Jim Bakker, as long as people are "stupid" enough to send it, they'll take the money.
3. They may seriously believe what they preach, but only Christ has and is the answer.
4. They believe in an extra-biblical revelation. For example, Joseph Smith, Mary Baker Eddy, Sun Yung Moon, Charles T. Russell.

    Russell claimed that the real gospel had never been preached until he came on the scene. Armstrong said that for the first time since A.D. 69, the true gospel of Jesus Christ had been preached—by him, of course. Mormons place Joseph Smith's writing on a higher plane than the Bible. They deny justification by faith and propose a system of works.
5. Most cults are fanatically hostile to the Bible as it now stands and to the divinity of Christ.
6. Most cults challenge the authority and accuracy of the Bible

in an attempt to prove either that it is not the infallible Word of God, or that it does not say what Christians generally believe it says.

Many of these cults contact pastors of conventional churches seeking opportunities to come and provide information about their organizations.

Strange as it may seem, most cults have basically the same general pattern or M.O.

Characteristics of cult teachings include the following:

1. A false or inadequate basis of salvation. "We, alone, have the truth, and there is salvation in no other outside our group."
2. A need for extra-biblical or additional revelations.
3. A false basis of authority. Followers must obey implicitly.
4. Salvation by works.
5. Most cult leaders claim to be in direct contact with spirit entities.
6. Most cults deny the reality of judgment and eternal punishment.

A Closer Look at Some Cults

The Mormon Church holds to four books: The Bible, *The Book of Mormon, Doctrines and Covenants,* and *The Pearl of Great Price.*

The Book of Mormon contains no philosophical or religious truths that are not stated much better elsewhere.

The average Mormon is not aware that Joseph Smith later contradicted his former "revelations" and that *The Book of Mormon, Doctrine and Covenants,* and *The Pearl of Great Price* have been secretly revised from time to time in order to accommodate changing Mormon doctrines.

Supposedly no one on the earth for 18 centuries knew the truth until Joseph Smith and some others came along with new revelations and "correct" interpretations.

Mormons sincerely believe that their faith is truly Biblical because their people claim to honor God's Word. However, every Mormon has been taught to say that he accepts the Bible only to the extent that it is "translated correctly." In practical terms this means that wherever the Bible contradicts Mormonism, there must be a mistake in the Bible.

The Book of Mormon was supposed to have been buried. It was found by Joseph Smith. Supposedly buried in AD 428, it contains words verbatim from the King James Version of the Bible (1611).

Mormons do not believe in the Virgin birth. They believe that Jesus was a polygamist, married to the two Marys and Martha. Andrew Jensen, assistant Church Historian, listed 27 women who were married to Joseph Smith.

Mormons believe in baptism for the dead.

To the Mormon, Joseph Smith became the gate-keeper to heaven.

Now for a glimpse of the Moon, the Unification Church.

On Easter morning in 1936, Sun Myung Moon, a Korean evangelist, claims that he had a vision at which time he heard Christ speak to him and urge him to carry out the mission that Jesus was not able to complete.

Since 1973 Moon has been a permanent resident of the USA. During these intervening years, he and his church have amassed a financial empire. But he has had serious difficulties with governmental agencies. He claims harassment and violation of his civil rights.

A set-back occurred July 16, 1982, when Moon was sentenced to 18 months in jail and a $25,000 fine for tax evasion. Moon was later released from prison. He held a press conference in 1985. Rev. Jerry Falwell, reportedly, took part and called on then President Reagan to issue a full pardon to Moon.

Moon is in open hostility to Christianity. He regards himself as the most important man alive. And he claims to be the prophet of the new age. His book, *The Divine Principle*, is his Bible.

Moon denies the Virgin Birth and the Trinity. He claims to be greater than Jesus Himself. "The whole world is in my hand," he claims, "and I will conquer and subjugate the world."

According to his doctrine, Jesus failed to marry and produce physical children and to establish the perfect family. So Moon, the new Messiah, and his wife, as father and mother of the perfect family, are doing what Jesus failed to do.

Moon's followers honor him as "father."

His church claims to be the only vehicle of salvation. Followers are taught that everybody not in the Moon movement is under the influence of Satan and should be distrusted.

According to Moon, "We are living in a new age which began in 1960."

One of the goals of the movement is the establishment of a world-wide government in which the separation of church and state would be abolished, and ALL WOULD BE GOVERNED BY MOON AND HIS FOLLOWERS.

Moon requires his believers to sacrifice everything to his cause. In return he guarantees: (1) A strong supportive community, (2) A powerful father figure, (3) All the necessities of life, and (4) Eternal salvation.

After she had been indoctrinated into Moon's Unification Church, Podee Forrester learned that her main function was to raise money. Orders were to "Go out on the streets and stay until you have raised your quota."

Other Pseudo-Christian religions of the West include: Jehovah's Witnesses, Theosophy, and Jesus Freaks.

Scientology is a combination of psychotherapy and the Catholic confession. It has been called "The world's largest organization of unqualified persons engaged in the practice of dangerous techniques which masquerade as mental telepathy." In "Today's Health" Magazine it was called "a dangerous cult which claims to help mentally or emotionally disturbed people for sizeable fees."

Its leader, L. Ron Hubbard, wrote *Dianetics* as an attempt to improve on psychology. His later development of Scientology was a step further into Eastern mysticism while still retaining a strong underlying influence from psychotherapy.

During an argument, H.W. Armstrong told his son: "I am the church."

Armstrong predicted that His Worldwide Church of God would be raptured to the ancient city of Petra, near the Dead Sea, in 1972. He also predicted that Christ would return to earth in 1975. Obviously both predictions were wrong.

According to a former director of computer processing for the Worldwide Church of God, no man had any right to question anything Armstrong did because he reported only to God.

No church member was allowed to question his use of funds, his doctrines, his abuse of power, or anything else he did.

Clarence E. Hobbs from Washington State has a group he calls "Friendship." He advocates "Sex with others to save your soul." Hobbs has a mysterious hold over his congregation. The county sheriff says, "It is surely not the typical church."

Transendental Meditation represents another threat to the Christian message. Led by Maharishi Mahesh Yogi, TM meets all kinds of needs. Just give 40 minutes a day and $55 to $125 to it.

TM is clearly built on the Hindu Scriptures. *Newsweek* has called it a "vague mixture of self therapy, Hindu teaching, and flower power."

One authority has said it is like a big aspirin tablet for the headache of unhappiness.

TM claims to be a way to reduce stress and tension, improve

health, increase productivity, give self-confidence, and reduce the need for drugs.

Maharishi means "great sage." Yogi means one who practices yoga.

The Beatles and many other entertainers gave it a boost.

Elizabeth Claire Prophet's Church Universal and Triumphant is another form of Hindu occultism with a heavy emphasis on spirit contacts mixed with Buddhism, gnosticism, Christian Science, Unity and others—a smorgasbord of psycho-spiritual deception.

From her headquarters, Prophet claims to maintain regular contacts with spirits of long dead gurus.

Iskon—International Society for Krishna Consciousness—is less well known than some of the other cults. They chant for hours. "Hare Krishna" followers are easily recognized by their shaved heads and saffron robes. At airports they sell books and beg. They are known to have raised two billion dollars at Los Angeles airport.

Their guru was A.C. Bhaktivedanta, who died in 1977. But his work goes on. The constant chanting is an invocation to Hindu deities, so it has spiritual implications. "Don't worry about material things," they say. But at airports their selling books and begging brings them thousand of dollars.

Eldridge Cleaver was involved in a number of religious and political cults. He noticed that

1. They were all sworn enemies of historic Christianity;
2. They all had an authoritarian leadership that claimed a monopoly on truth;
3. They all demanded unquestioned obedience.

No cult would last very long if its members were allowed and encouraged to seek the truth by studying God's Word by itself without their peculiar interpretation.

A few of these groups are fairly new. Some are very small. But, remember, People's Temple (Jim Jones) was small in 1978.

Bahai is related to Islam. Bahaullah claimed to be the spirit of truth. He claimed to be Jesus Christ come back again.

The Bahai religion began in 1844 when a 24-year-old wool merchant took the title Bab and began preaching that he was the Messiah. The movement was actually founded in 1863.

Bahai collides head-on with Christianity. Jesus Christ claims to be the unique Son of God; the Way, the Truth, and the Life. He said, "No one comes to the Father, but by Me."

His followers declared, "Neither is there salvation in any other," and "There is one God and one Mediator between God and man." That Mediator is Jesus Christ.

It is one thing to accept the moral and ethical teaching of Bahaullah; it is quite another thing to accept him as the ultimate manifestation of God, the only way of salvation.

Toynbee has compared the unusually fast growth of Bahai to that of Christianity in the Roman Empire. He predicts that it might become the religion of world unity in the future.

Shortly before the Iranian hostage crisis, seven college students from Iran ate Thanksgiving dinner in our home. After dinner, assuming they were all Muslims, Art asked some questions about their faith.

That opened a Pandora's box. Several were Bahai followers. A heated argument erupted among them. One became especially upset because he wasn't sufficiently fluent in English to express himself. We listened in silence. They all left as friends to return to the apartments they shared. The main thing we learned was never to assume anything and never to discuss religion among strangers.

Today Eckankar is believed to be one of the largest social-religious fringe groups in the United States, if not in the world. Its estimated membership is 50,000. A multimillion dollar organization, it sells literature, jewelry, tapes, and membership dues. Its base is Menlo Park, California. It's a "Made in America" religion.

Its founder, Paul Twitchell, is proclaimed as Messiah. The group focuses on occult philosophy, mystical experience, and mind control.

Eckankar teaches that a soul enters the universe as a mineral and works its way up through plant, fish, reptile, and mammal incarnations. When it eventually becomes a human, it will spend any number of lifetimes until it attains spiritual enlightenment through Eckankar.

Twitchell realized that if he wanted to create a new religion, he had to conjure up a new concept of God to go with it. That was "We do not, and can not know God."

EST is a marriage between psychology and Eastern Mysticism. The *est* experience is designed, for a substantial fee, to shock a person out of his complacent existence into taking control, as God, of his own life. It teaches that a personal God is a myth, that the self is the only God.

Like Mormonism, Islam professes to accept the Bible, both Old and New Testaments. Like Joseph Smith, Mohammed claimed that the Bible had been deliberately corrupted by the scribes until it was so distorted that a new revelation was needed. What *The Book of Mormon* accomplished for Joseph Smith, the *Koran* accomplished for Mohammad. It was proclaimed as a "new revelation!"

Islam means "surrender, or submission to the will of Allah." *Muslim* means "one who submits."

Muslims reckon their calendar from Mohammed's flight to Mecca.

They claim Allah as the one true god. They say God never had a son. He has sent many prophets, including Jesus, but Mohammad was the last and the greatest.

Of the four inspired books they accept the *Koran* as the most important. Others they consider inspired are the *Pentatuch, Psalms,* and *The Evangel of Jeses.*

Islam teaches that there are many angels or intermediary spirits and that there will be a day of judgment, a heaven and a hell.

Five pillars of Islamic faith are (1) recite Islam's creed; (2) pray facing Mecca five times a day—upon rising, noon, mid-afternoon, sunset, and upon retiring; (3) give alms; (4) observe a month of fasting—Ramadan; and (5) make a pilgrimage to Mecca.

In a book by Samuel M. Zwemer (1940), he claimed "the religion of Islam is slowly disintegrating. Islam has been severely wounded in the house of its friends."

"Some tell us," he added "that there are signs of a resurgent Islam and a revival of faith in Mohammed, but all signs point in the opposite direction." That was 1940.

Today Islam is one of the most formidable enemies of Christianity. There are 7 million members in the USA. That number is increasing at an alarming rate.

According to *The New Columbia Encyclopedia*, "Various reasons for the rapid growth have been given; one, probably not the most potent, is the idea that he who dies fighting for the faith goes to paradise."

In the late 70's one of my Muslim friends loaned me a copy of his *Koran*. When I returned it to him, I said, "This says Muslims are supposed to kill Christians. Would you kill me?'"

After 09/11/01, Hal Lindsey, reportedly, said those who claim Muslims are not out to kill Christians haven't read the *Koran*. I didn't hear Lindsey say that, but I certainly agree.

I did hear Franklin Graham, son of Dr. Billy Graham, say that they don't serve the same God we do. Obviously they don't. Our God has a Son; Allah doesn't have a son.

Perhaps Satan's most cunning device is the one-world church movement gaining support at incredible speed among some of the most incredible religions. If we're not vigilant we may be swept up in this trap of the devil.

While our country was founded on freedom—including freedom of religion—as Christians we dare not condone any "religion" that does not worship Jesus Christ. Granted, Jesus taught us to love our enemies. But no one ever spoke more blistering words than Jesus spoke to and about the religious leaders of His day.

Had He and His disciples exercised tolerance to the extent that we're encouraged to do today, they could have died a natural death.

If it ever becomes necessary, let's pray that we will follow their example. "There is no other name under heaven whereby we must be saved" (Acts 4:12).

Our best defense against false religions is not argument. It is simply stating in no uncertain terms that we follow the teachings of Jesus only and we don't need anyone else to lead us. Jesus is the one and only way.

CHAPTER 9

Hints for Improving Relationships

Men and women enter the ministry for a variety of reasons. Parental pressure propels some. A pastor-hero's influence lures others. The myth of a fabulous salary for one or two hour's work per week perhaps entices a few.

From each of these ranks, however, come a host of dropouts. Glamour may sustain human motivation during the pastoral honeymoon. But, when pastor and laymen become aware of each other's faults, the honeymoon is over. Then a pastor needs Saint Paul's compelling, "Woe is me if I preach not the gospel," to keep from resigning every Sunday night.

An alarming number of churches are experiencing a serious shortage of pastors every year because so many leave the pastorate.

Keeping romance alive requires the cooperation of both partners. Too often, in the church as well as in a marriage, a spirit of competition for power mars the joy and success of the partnership. Without an attitude of tolerance, the cause nearest the heart of both partners suffers.

Because people have problems, churches have problems. Thus the church needs more than a preacher; it needs a pastor—one with the wisdom and foresight to prevent trouble, the love and tact to cope with it, the faith and patience to endure it, and, above all, the ability and determination not to precipitate nor aggravate it.

I have read scores of books and hundreds of articles written by ministers. I have listened to high ranking church officials offer practical advice to pastors. I have yet to hear in public or see in print one layman's views on how a pastor can improve performance.

With all due respect to the ministry, surely an active, loyal layman, with a lifetime of service has some practical ideas that might well increase the pastor's effectiveness.

This is the voice of a partner in ministry, who helps pay the pastor's salary, who glories in the pastor's successes, and who picks up the pieces when the pastor fails. It is designed to enable the pastor to be more productive in God's kingdom.

When You Arrive

Forget the past. You have prayed about this move. Now accept it as God's will. Whether you experienced success or failure in your last pastorate, this one is different.

Act enthusiastic. Dale Carnegie said if you act enthusiastic, you'll be enthusiastic.

Accept the church:
The Parsonage
   The Salary
      The Building
         The Congregation
            The Community
               The Challenge
                  The Responsibility

Abrupt changes scare most people; avoid making too many too soon. Proceed with caution. But try to make changes for the better as soon as practicable.

Ignore the informers. Some former pastors and lay tattlers who consider it their sacred duty to pass on their knowledge and prejudices, often hinder your faith and your influence in your new assignment. Refuse to make snap judgments on the basis of second-hand information.

When You Preach

Preach the Word. No other sermon is worthy of the name. No one was ever called to preach his convictions.

Know what the Bible teaches and what your church believes. Your congregation has a right to expect you to preach the doctrines of its denomination. If you cannot adhere to those teachings, join another denomination or start one of your own.

Avoid public censorship of your denominational leaders and institutions. Go through proper channels to protest improper conduct or unorthodox theology. But, at all costs, don't risk offending a weak Christian or an outsider by criticizing someone in your own ranks. A house divided against itself cannot stand; neither can a church.

Study. Your congregation has a right to expect you to be informed.

Relate Bible truths to the present. Make the Bible come alive, or your audience won't.

Preach with Authority. Never apologize for Bible truth nor church tenets. Understand the reason for church standards and defend them.

Preach with Love. Your job is to feed, not skin, the sheep. Don't take out your frustrations on your congregation. They have their own problems. If you're ill or upset, stay at home. Ask someone else to preach or ask a layman to take charge. The Lord only knows how much damage a pastor can do when he "just isn't feeling up to par."

Preach with Unction. Without the Holy Spirit to speak through you, what you say will do very little good. Wait before God in Bible reading, meditation, and prayer until He anoints you to preach. One highly successful preacher said he never preached a sermon without two hours of prayer behind it.

Preach with Confidence. Don't be afraid of people. You take your orders from God, not from your official board nor from other prominent members. But don't preach at people or try to offend them. Your messages will disturb enough listeners without a deliberate attempt to do so.

Use good English. Today's educational opportunities leave absolutely no excuse for illiteracy in the pulpit. If necessary, buy a grammar textbook and master it. Ask someone in your audience—your spouse, your children, or some understanding friend—to call your attention to errors that you make consistently. Anyone will make an occasional error. But few listeners can fail to tune out the pastor who consistently misuses his language.

One pastor I knew consistently used malapropisms. When calling the congregation to prayer, for example, he said, "We can convene to God what we can't convene to anyone else" or "Let's pray much and not be too friculous." Yet he expressed his disappointment to us that his district superintendent didn't give him a larger church.

You would likely have no more that a half dozen of grammatical errors to correct. You owe it to yourself, your family, your audience, and Christ to rid yourself of such obstacles to effective preaching.

Enlarge your vocabulary. Forceful language involves the use of numerous synonyms to prevent repetition. Ask your spouse to give you a copy of Roget's *Thesaurus* or use the one in your computer as an aid to more effective, more stimulating sermons.

Improve your Voice. Avoid a monotone. Speak loud enough, but don't yell. If people have hearing problems, hearing aids are available. If you stand too near a microphone, your words sound garbled; if you stand too far away, your words are indistinct. If you move back and forth too much, you sound like a radio with a weak tube. Ask listeners in both front and back pews to help gauge your volume. A woman's ears are more sensitive than a man's; include a lady in your volume opinion poll.

Guage your speed. Dragging a sermon or the entire service as if waiting for the Rapture is one extreme. Speeding through like a TV announcer is the other. Your audience should be able to follow your message but not to relax too much.

Sing softly if you can't carry a tune, No choir can drown out an enthusiastic, tone-deaf pastor. Yet no layman dares hint that the beloved zealous minister ruins the song service.

Dress in Good Taste. Your congregation has a right to expect neatness, good grooming, cleanliness, and appropriateness in your person and your attire. You represent God and His Kingdom. Dress the part.

When You Pray

Every sincere Christian recognizes the importance of prayer as a means of sustaining his relationship with God. But praying long elaborate prayers is not necessarily a sign of Christianity. Devotees of other religions often put Christians to shame in the time spent in prayer and the intensity of those prayers. Although he sees no benefit from praying to any other god, the Christian admits that his spiritual life depends upon prayer.

The disciples' request, "Lord, teach us to pray," should be the heart cry of every Christian. Neither a filler nor a form, prayer contributes to or detracts from a service. The pastor largely determines which.

Do most of your praying in secret. Avoid praying long prayers in public to compensate for lack of private prayer.

Become so well acquainted with the Lord that you don't have to read your prayers. Can you imagine a lover calling his beloved and saying, "Just a minute, Sweetheart, I have written down what I want to say"?

Your prayer should impress the Lord with your devotion and sincerity; what the audience thinks of it is immaterial. The public prayer that touches God will touch an audience, whether the language be polished or crude.

Ordinarily the Pastoral Prayer in the Sunday morning worship service gives the pastor an excellent opportunity to pray for his people and present their needs and concerns to the Lord. With a personal acquaintance with God and with the congregation, the compassionate pastor can bring the two together in a hallowed relationship which makes a worship service something special.

One of the most meaningful times in the church which I attend is a special Sunday morning prayer time. Our pastor invites anyone from the congregation who wishes to come to the altar to pray about anything. As the people come with all their needs, the pastor kneels on the other side of the altar and prays his pastoral prayer.

Since a very creative pastor started this practice some twenty-five years ago, prayer time has become a high point in every Sunday morning service.

When You Visit the Sick

Pleasant or unpleasant, one important aspect of a pastor's responsibility is visiting the sick. The illness of a church member often gives the pastor a unique opportunity to minister to the unchurched as well. The effectiveness of those encounters depends on the pastor's attitude and behavior.

A highly successful hospital caller offers the following suggestions:

1. Enter quietly and compassionately.
2. Don't ask a lot of questions.
3. Make the call short. They will have other visitors.
4. When the doctor comes in, you go out.
5. Always respect a closed door.
6. When the nurse comes in, excuse yourself.
7. Avoid touching a bed. Avoid sitting. You'll stay too long.
8. Keep the conversation positive. Bad news has no place there.
9. Though you ordinarily pray with them there are times when you should not. Always assure them of your prayers. Notify the proper people.
10. Include the person next to them in the prayer. Meet that person if he/she is alert.
11. If patient is in ICU, go to the waiting room. Meet with family. If not there, give card to nurse to give to patient or family. Make visit short.
12. The family has priority. Be sensitive when a spouse comes.
13. When you pray, pray "softly and tenderly."

14. Never whisper about the patient's condition in a room with the family.
15. Remember you are representing God and the church.
16. Try not to visit on Sunday afternoon. That's when everyone else comes.

You probably already observe these suggestions. I hope you will pass them along to your laymen.

Hospital visitors play an important role in the welfare of a patient. Under the right circumstances they let the patient know someone cares; they boost morale; they help to pass the time; and their prayers mean everything.

Personal experience has convinced me that failure to be sensitive to the situation, however, may do more harm than good. A few years ago I was in the hospital for two months with a one percent chance to live. Some three score friends came to pray with me. Their visits and prayers meant everything to me.

Unfortunately, one Sunday night when I was in ICU fighting for my life, barely able to breathe, much less talk, three couples from my Sunday school class appeared. I remember saying, "O no!" to myself when I saw that host at my door. Don't ask me how they got in. They sensed the situation and left.

Without the prayers of those friends and scores of others of course, I wouldn't be here. But, as Solomon tells us, there's a time for everything.

When You Plan

Any pastor worth a salary spends much time in planning. Just as plans for any organization are subject to the approval of its chief executive, so church plans must have God's approval if they are to succeed. Combine prayer with logical thinking, your own and that of others.

Be willing to listen to others. Share the credit with others. Consult department heads, committees, or whoever has responsibility for a particular phase before setting your plan in operation. If you have a youth leader, share your plan with him and ask him for suggestions. Your missionary president will cooperate more willingly if you consult him/her about missionary planning. Your song leader appreciates your consulting him about plans for the music program.

Be willing to change your plans if they aren't acceptable. Be patient. Resist the urge to try to change everything overnight. That brilliant idea you used to such advantage in your former pastorate might not work at all in your present church.

A pastor who cooperates readily seldom has difficulty getting laymen to cooperate.

When You Have a Board Meeting

Announce board meetings well in advance. Specify a time to begin and to end. Plan the agenda and, if possible, notify board members ahead of time concerning important matters to be discussed. Stick to the agenda. Keep things moving. Keep control. Refuse to let one or two members monopolize the time.

Know parliamentary procedure. Be charitable and insist that others be charitable toward differences of opinion. After all, no one's judgment is infallible.

Reject the tendency to take every disagreement as a personal offense. Few people have mastered the art of disagreeing yet remaining friends with an opponent. Teach your members that differences are inevitable and often beneficial provided everyone—including the pastor—recognizes the rights of others to their opinions.

Someone has said that if two business partners agree on everything, one of them is unnecessary. Paul and Barnabas had a disagreement. It resulted in two missionary parties, instead of one. Paul withstood Peter to his face because of Peter's inconsistency regarding his attitude toward the Gentiles. With charity and good judgment, you can help your church board to survive and even thrive on differences.

When You Participate in Community Affairs

Take advantage of opportunities to represent Christ and your church in community affairs.

Join the ministerial alliance. Attend the meetings. Be willing to serve as an officer or committee member. If you can't conscientiously cooperate in some areas, admit that you can't and tactfully explain why. Don't compromise essentials, but be charitable. Emphasize points of agreement; minimize differences.

Urge your members to attend special union services; then make yourself conspicuous for your presence, not for your absence. When your official board votes to dismiss regular services to encourage everyone to participate in union meetings, it is not a vote to give the pastor that time off. Avoid embarrassing your laymen by forcing them to explain, "Our pastor is out of town." The fact that you may be unable to cooperate in some programs makes it the more imperative that you actively participate whenever you can.

Pastors who take an active part in community affairs not only enlarge their own congregations, but they also exert a far greater influence for God.

One middle-aged carpenter-turned-preacher accepted a "challenge" and moved his family of five children into the church basement. With a dilapidated building, fewer than fifty church members—most of them elderly, some widows—a salary of $6.00 per week, this devoted parson's family set to work.

While their children attended school, the pastor and his wife worked at carpentry and interior decorating to supplement their salary.

Lack of formal education, a small congregation, undesirable living conditions, meager salary resulting in manual labor would have intimidated a lesser man. But not this pastor.

He associated with businessmen, doctors, lawyers, educators, fellow ministers and won their respect and confidence. Invitations to participate in various community events came with increasing frequency.

Young people and children swarmed into the basement parsonage for fellowship with each other and the pastor's children. Enthusiastic voices drowned out sour notes coming from a banged-up piano. Climbing the steps into church seemed the next logical step. Church and Sunday school attendance increased, and the congregation took on a new look.

He accepted five public school teachers into the church. At least one, yours truly, owed her job to the influence of this pastor in the community.

As his congregation and salary increased, he devoted less time to secular work, He moved an old house in and made it into a comfortable parsonage, and he left the church, for a better one, knowing that the community respected the church much more than when he came. He laid a good foundation.

A few years later, that church called another pastor who won his way into the hearts of the townspeople and built a beautiful church and parsonage; established a strong, stable congregation; and reached out into surrounding communities with his influence for Christ. He attended almost every respectable event in the community. He might speak, pray, or help with the public address system; but everyone knew he was there. He stayed thirty-five or forty years.

Surely a pastor's responsibility extends beyond the border of his local membership. The pastor has much to contribute to the community. God help him if he fails to make that contribution.

When You Receive an Offering

Some denominations elect or appoint laymen to handle the financial affairs of the church. In many others, however, raising money constitutes part of the pastor's responsibility. The pastor's attitude largely determines whether taking an offering challenges or terrifies both pastor and congregation.

At the risk of being known as one who preaches for money, teach your people that giving is a vital part of worship. "God loves a cheerful giver." Surely then, God detests a stingy giver or one who doesn't give at all.

Jesus called special attention to a poor widow who gave all she had and to an affectionate Mary, who poured costly ointment on the Master's feet. Giving goes hand in hand with loving: "God so loved . . . that he gave . . ." If a man loves the Lord, he gives willingly, not grudgingly, to support God's work.

Avoid apologies. The cashier in a grocery store or in a restaurant would lose her job if she apologized to a customer for asking for money. When the customer has a basket or stomach full of good food, he doesn't complain about the cost. A well balanced spiritual diet greatly reduces complaints about offerings—and everything else.

Emphasize positive aspects of generous giving, but don't browbeat church members who fail to respond. Only God knows their hearts and their financial status. Some conscientious Christians refuse to pledge money to the church although they habitually pledge money to a bank or loan company to buy a new car. Others say they don't want their right hand to know what their left hand is doing—usually their left hand isn't doing anything. Whatever the excuse, God does not force people to give; neither can the pastor.

Don't gauge your giving by that of others. Some pastors hesitate to give more than laymen give. Others almost bankrupt themselves trying to give as much as their highest-paying members. The layman who gives the largest amount may have less expense and more income—even more faith—than others. Set an example, but don't let the people regulate your giving.

Taking an offering is like selling: enthusiasm usually precludes success. You must be sold on the project if your congregation supports it.

Pray about the offering. Alert your people and ask them to pray. Present the need enthusiastically, expectantly, and unapologetically. Convince your church of the blessings of giving. Extend the opportunity to everyone, even young people and children. You'll be surprised at the response.

When You Have a Family

If you are typical you either have a spouse or you are looking for one.

Since most pastors are men let's talk about the pastor's wife.

Like every wife since Eve, a pastor's wife should be a helpmeet. She helps him meet appointments, responsibilities, and expenses. She need not be a Miss America, but as Queen of your parsonage, she needs charm and poise. She must be an efficient housekeeper. It helps if she can play the organ or piano, and cook. She must be a sympathetic listener, a financial wizard, and a competent psychologist. She must love you or some other woman will. She should have confidence in herself, in you, in your church members, and in God.

No matter how nearly perfect your wife may be, some members with magnifying glasses can find faults. Refuse to try to mold your wife into everyone's ideal. She has a right to be an individual. Encourage her to dress in good taste and to conduct herself like a lady, but don't expect more of her than you expect of other ladies in your church. Make her consider that being a pastor's wife is a privilege.

Love and respect your wife. Be her best booster. She can face criticism, loneliness, and deprivation if she knows you love and appreciate her. Marriage means more to her than it does to you. Your life may be the ministry; hers is her marriage.

Schedule time to forget you're a minister. You will live longer and your marriage with thrive. You married a woman, not your church. One pastor designated Monday night as church family night. A few weeks later his wife said, "*You* aren't taking Monday nights for *your* family." He would say, "I'd better go see the _____ family; this is the only night I can catch them at home." No doubt that family wanted a family night too.

Don't let the church make a slave of your wife. Some congregations expect the pastor's wife to play the organ or piano, direct or sing in the choir, supervise vacation Bible school, teach a Sunday school class, serve as missionary president—you name it. Discourage her election to more positions than other church women fill. Granted, she may be better qualified than others; nevertheless, she can experience burnout.

Try to keep her off the church board. Every loyal wife will defend her husband. Such defense in a board meeting can be devastating. Although not a board member, one elderly pastor's wife regularly participated in board meetings. No one objected until one night she voted on a highly controversial issue. The pastor voted off the tie.

When the secretary of the board dared ask the pastor to read from the manual a list of board members, the pastor exploded. "I presume you are referring to Mrs. _____. That's the first time in all of my ministry that her vote has been questioned."

No amount of salve could heal the wounds of that board meeting. The pastor called no more board meetings during the next six months of his tenure. Fortunately, all the board members remained friends.

Provide your wife and family with necessities and some luxuries. If secular employment becomes necessary, consider working part time to avoid depriving your family. Jesus worked in Joseph's carpenter shop; Paul worked as a tentmaker.

Some ministers have lost their souls by trying to serve "God and mammon." Others have lost their families by refusing to do secular labor to support them. Only much prayer and divine wisdom can enable a pastor to maintain a proper balance.

Get some relaxation—and sleep. Keep physically fit. Discipline yourself and your children.

Be careful what you say about other people's children, because you may have to eat your words when yours grow up.

Teach your children to love and respect the church. Guard your tongue. Some pastors have lost their children to the church because of gossip about church members. Respect confidential information. Surely a minister should be as ethical as a doctor or an attorney.

Refuse to let your children become pawns of the church. More than a few ministers have driven their children away from the church by demanding paragons of perfection—often to satisfy the pastor's ego as well as some member's ideal of "a preacher's kid."

Make your family glad you are a pastor. When you must deprive your family of a cherished possession or activity, provide an alternate of equal or greater pleasure. Thus you reduce the risk of a martyr complex.

Families of men in other professions make certain sacrifices. The minister's family is no exception. But whether his family sacrifices willingly depends largely upon the attitude of the minister toward his work.

Paul's advice to Timothy concerning a bishop and his family serves as a model for any minister.

When You Have Money Problems

A district superintendent said he always looked for three characteristics in a pastor: (1) Ability to preach, (2) A Shepherd's heart, and (3) Business ability. "With two of these," he continued, "he will be very successful; with one, he will make it; with all three, the sky's the limit!"

You will likely have dreamers and plodders in your church. You need enough business sense, coupled with diplomacy, to lead your church forward without plunging them hopelessly in debt. Reject the temptation to use other people's money more recklessly than your own.

Budget your personal finances wisely. Be honest. Expect no handouts because you're a preacher. Pay your way.

Pay your bills promptly. Only God knows how much damage pastors have caused by failing to pay their bills. No doubt most pastors fully intend to pay, but one failure makes it easy to start a pattern.

Cleaning the church one night, a couple found a waste basket into which the pastor had emptied his desk drawers before moving after dark the night before. That stack of papers included several hot checks, thousands of dollars worth of unpaid notes, and a cancelled insurance policy on the car he drove out of state, pulling a trailer load of mortgaged furniture. He was soon out of the ministry. But the church never recuperated from his indiscretion.

When You Disagree with a Layman

Examine your motives and your attitude. Don't throw up your hands in despair. Don't assume automatically that the layman is wrong. Find points on which you agree and major on those. If you become sufficiently well acquainted with your opponent, you might even win him to your side or be won to his.

Be firm on essentials but tolerant of nonessentials. Jesus said, "Agree with thine adversary quickly whilst thou art in the way with him." As long as you are the pastor and that layman is your parishioner, you will be "in the way with him." If you two don't learn to agree, or at least to disagree agreeably, you will both be "in the way" of others.

Avoid the temptation to run to other laymen to enlist their support. A person who tries to destroy another usually destroys himself and enhances his opponent. Whatever you do, resist the cowardly temptation to take out your hostilities in the pulpit where your opposition can't reply. Such behavior is far beneath the dignity of an ambassador for Christ.

If a serious dispute threatens to split the church, you may have to resign.

When You Leave

Most pastors who have made a substantial contribution to a church have had long-term pastorates. Most churches that have made substantial progress have had long-term pastors.

When the time comes for you to leave, however, stifle your emotions, encourage your people, leave and break any ties that will interfere with the work of your successor.

CHAPTER 10

A Crash Course in Communications

No matter how much you know about sermon material if you can't get it across to your listeners, it's of little value. Designed to pep up your style, the following tips are guaranteed to enhance your performance. They apply equally to writing and speaking.

For best results, keep them in mind and work them into your sermons *gradually*.

I. Consider Writer's Digest School's "Rules for Good Writing:"

    A. Prefer the plain word to the fancy.
    B. Prefer the familiar word to the unfamiliar.
    C. Prefer the Saxon word to the Romance.
    D. Prefer nouns and verbs to adjectives and adverbs.
    E. Prefer picture nouns and action verbs.
    F. Never use a long word when a short one will do as well.
    G. Master the simple declarative sentence.
    H. Prefer the simple sentence to the complicated.
    I. Vary your sentence length.
    J. Put the words you want to emphasize at the beginning or end of your sentence.
    K. Use the active voice. Make your subject *do* something.
    L. Put statements in a positive form.
    M. Use short paragraphs.
    N. Cut needless words, sentences, and paragraphs.
    O. Use plain, conversational language. Write like you talk.

P. Avoid imitation. Write in your natural style.
Q. Write clearly.
R. Write to be understood, not to impress.
S. Revise and rewrite.

   Oklahoma State University English Professor Jack Campbell said, "There's no such thing as good writing; it's good rewriting."

II. Consider what your reader/listener demands.

   A. Appeal to my emotions.

      1. Make me cry.
      2. Make me laugh.
      3. Make me shudder.
      4. Make me cringe.
      5. Make me mad.

   B. Appeal to my senses.

      1. Make me see.
      2. Make me smell.
      3. Make me taste.
      4. Make me hear.
      5. Make me feel (touch).

   C. Appeal to my interests

      1. Tell me what I don't know.
      2. Tell me what I want to know.
      3. Tell me what *you* know.
      4. Tell me why I should know.
      5. Make me want to know.

   D. Appeal to my intellect.

1. Make me think.
2. Make me reason.
3. Make me understand.
4. Make me respond.
5. Make me empathize.

III. Paint word pictures.

   A. Figures of Speech
   Our everyday speech is peppered with figurative language. We can hardly open our mouths without using it. Such expressions as "sky high," "as wide as the ocean," "as deep as the sea," "picture perfect," "as stubborn as a mule," "as dirty as a hog," "as clumsy as a cow," "eats like a pig," or a thousand others, comprise much of our conversation.

   The Bible abounds in examples of figures of speech.

   In Ecclesiates 12, Solomon uses metaphor to give an unforgettable picture of old age: loss of zest for life, trembling hands, arthritic knees, loss of teeth, failing eyesight, loss of hearing, and insomnia.

   In the 23rd Psalm, David uses the metaphor of the shepherd and the sheep to convey his relationship to God. As a shepherd, he could relate to that concept. That's the best known of all the Psalms because it portrays how God cares for His own.

   Jesus, the Master story teller, picks up on David's picture. For example, "I am the Good Shepherd" and the story of the "Lost Sheep."

   Jesus uses the comparison of His relationship to us in such expressions as "I am the Bread of life," "I am the Way, the truth, and the life." He describes his followers as "the light of the world," or "the salt of the earth,"

   Much of the Book of Luke consists of parables which Jesus told to explain His teachings. The disciples didn't always understand. Often Jesus had to explain the parable. Even then sometimes they didn't understand.

Because we don't always understand figurative language, we have different views and scores of denominations. One group takes a figure of speech literally; another takes it figuratively. But if we should take it out of the teachings of Jesus, we would have little left.

Such Chinese proverbs as "Sooner or later we will all sit down to a banquet of consequences" and "When the day is as dark as the night, it is better to light a candle than to curse the darkness" paint vivid pictures of truth.

As forceful as figurative language is, however, overuse reduces its effectiveness. Like chewing gum, it loses its flavor. Blessed is the pastor who can think of fresh images.

Everyone uses metaphor. Unfortunately, not everyone can interpret it.

That's when we need illustrations.

B. Illustrations

Doubtless the sermons you remember are those with striking pictures.

As a teenager, I watched an evangelist at a camp meeting in the foothills of the Ozarks illustrate the trouble a cantankerous church member can cause. He compared that member to a mule with one foot over the trace. Then he dramatized the scene.

I'm not recommending such antics for most preachers in most situations. Though raised on the farm, this one was no hillbilly. But, like Jesus, he knew how to fit the illustration to his listeners. That congregation knew exactly how a mule looked trying to walk with one foot over the trace and how frustrating it was. After 65 years, I can still see that preacher hobbling around on the crude platform under that tabernacle.

On another occasion, by portraying an anxious

Hebrew lad frequently reminding his father that the blood must be on the door post before midnight, one evangelist gave his audience an unforgettable close-up of the plight of the eldest son on the night of Israel's departure from Egypt.

As the sun sank lower and lower, the boy's anxiety and his father's carelessness kept listeners alert and sympathetic. Few could forget the story of the Passover and the significance of the father's neglect.

After more than forty years, I still remember that sermon.

C. Verbs

1. We learned in elementary school that adjectives and adverbs describe. They do. But verbs paint a much clearer picture.

   For example: "I saw a man going down the street." Of course we need some adjectives to describe the man—"a long-haired middle aged, 150 lb. white man." And we need other adjectives to describe the street—"East Main Street." But the verbs really paint the picture.

   "I saw a long-haired, middle aged, 150 lb., white man jogging—hobbling, shuffling, groping, tottering, staggering, driving, pedaling, strolling, walking, crawling, streaking, sneaking, ambling, racing—down East Main Street." You can think of others. Each gives us a different picture.

   The more vivid the image you create, the more your audience will come alive. Appeal to as many of the five senses as possible to create those images.

2. Make your subject *do* something. a. Avoid passive voice except when the subject is a victim. Journalists use passive voice extensively because their subject is

often a victim. For example, "A child was hit by a truck" is passive voice. "A truck hit a child" is active voice. b. Wherever possible, avoid all forms of the verb "to be." Those are verbs of existence, not of action. If you can rephrase the sentence to avoid "is," "are," "were," "has been," "will be," or other passive verbs, it will come alive. c. Avoid the word "there" except when it refers to place. "There were thirty children in the classroom" could be "Thirty eighth-graders swarmed into the tiny classroom." d. Use as few words as possible to convey your meaning. Reduce a clause to a phrase, a phrase to a one-or two-word modifier. And place that modifier as close as possible to the word it modifies. One of the most frequent errors is the dangling participle. "Walking down the hall, the music could be heard." The music isn't walking down the hall; we are. "Walking down the hall, we could hear music." e. Prefer the affirmative. For example, in my final revision of the Chapter 9, I deliberately looked for the word "Don't." In *most* cases I was able to avoid it and make the statement more palatable.

IV. Strive for sentence variety.

- A. Use various kinds: simple, complex, compound; declarative, interrogative, imperative, exclamatory. Use exclamatory sentences sparingly.
- B. Use periodic sentences *occasionally* for effect. "We'll never know who the culprit was." "Who the culprit was, we'll never know." In other words, save the main clause until the end.
- C. Vary the length of sentences. Practice the rhythm of speech.

    Lucile Vaughan Payne says, "All spoken language, no matter who the speaker may be or what his subject is, has a natural rhythm. You will hear this rhythm wherever you hear talk: in your best friend's conversation, in a salesman's pitch, in a math teacher's explanation of a problem, in an impromptu speech at a club meeting, in your father's reading of the riot act.

"Compare the two short paragraphs below.
"Example A

"I want that car back here by ten o'clock. And when I say ten o'clock, I don't mean ten-thirty or ten-fifteen or ten-five. I mean *ten*. Because I'm telling you right now, this is the last time you drive that car if you come home late again. And that's final!
"Example B

"One of the things that is very important to an actor is a sense of timing. It is more important than a handsome face or a good voice. An actor who does not have a sense of timing can never be very good at acting. A good director can tell him what to do, but he will always be just like a puppet.

"Few things are so essential to an actor as a sense of timing. Without that, nothing else about him matters very much. He may have a handsome face. He may have a splendid voice. But unless he has an innate sense of timing, the finest director in the world cannot make an actor of him. He can never be more than a puppet.

"The second paragraph is more effective because the sentences now have the natural rhythm of speech. In fact, the rhythm of the second paragraph is a deliberate repetition of the rhythm of the father's natural speech.

The first principle of rhythm in writing, to capture the basic rhythm of speech, is variation of sentence length."*

**The Lively Art of Writing,* Follett Educational Corporation, Chicago, Ill., 1970, pp.123-125.

V. Pronounce words correctly.

The following "tell" of woe is an example of what I hear, especially on TV, where reporters should know how to pronounce the long *a* sound.

1. "The suspect is a white mell."
2. "He got out of jell on bell."
3. "The sell ends April 30."
4. "The driver felled to make it across the rellroad tracks."
5. "Stay tuned for further detells."
6. "Your check is in the mell."
7. "The infant received third-degree burns when she pulled a pell of hot water off the stove."
8. "We can expect strong winds and hell."
9. "Mr. Jones was belling hay when his dog's tell got caught in the beller."

That's only an example of the error that grates on my ears the most.

Of course, our mother tongue influences the language of us all. In addition, Bible names pose some difficulty. But public speakers who frequently mispronounce words tend to turn listeners off.

VI. Eliminate pet expressions.

Everyone has certain words or phrases that characterize his speech. But not everyone speaks to the same audience for an hour at one sitting week after week.

A popular television newscaster remarked to a colleague, "You haven't said, 'Fantastic' for two weeks."

The most frequently used, senseless, boring, and time-consuming pet expression is "You know." When most athletes appear on TV, 90% of the interview—at least it seems like that much time—is composed of "You know." A friend of mine with a Ph.D. Degree can hardly open her mouth without saying "You know." One preacher I know often muffles it under his breath, not only at the beginning or end of almost every sentence, but often in the middle.

When I hear that expression, I feel like saying what Judge Wapner used to say on "The People's Court." If a defendant said, "You know," the Judge would say, "No, I don't know."

Resorting to that expression betrays the fact that the speaker has failed to prepare adequately. He stalls for time because he doesn't know what to say next.

How many sermons can you preach without using your pet expression(s)?

VII. Be alert to mannerisms.

Mannerisms, such as brushing your hair back, taking off and putting on your glasses, tugging at your clothes, putting your hand in your pocket, and any number of other nervous habits, irritate your most ardent admirers and distract from your message.

God has called you to proclaim His message to the world that desperately needs it. As long as you are in partnership with Him, you cannot fail. May God help you as you continue to fulfill His mission for your life.

If something you've read in this book aids you in that endeavor, it will have accomplished its purpose.

May God's richest blessings rest upon you as you continue to follow God's plan for your life in one of the most difficult, yet one of the most important and rewarding, of His assignments.

BVG